# OVERLAND

## *Remembering Southeast Asia*

# CARYN GREEN

MANITOU & CEDAR PRESS

CHICAGO, ILLINOIS

2018

*OVERLAND: REMEMBERING SOUTHEAST ASIA* ~ © 2018
Caryn Green
All rights reserved
Published in the United States of America
Manitou & Cedar Press.


ISBN-13: 978-0-6926635-6-1

LIBRARY OF CONGRESS CONTROL NUMBER: 2018904809

This is a work of non-fiction. Any resemblance to actual persons, living or dead, places, events or incidents, is entirely intentional.

Photographs: Copyright © 2017 CN Green
Cover: *Hua Ta Non, Koh Samui: 25 Jan, 1976*
Frontispiece: *Jalan Malioboro, Jogjakarta: 7 Dec, 1975*


Cover and book design by Himanshu J. Suthar, GoldenMoonDesign.com

For my parents –
of blessed memory

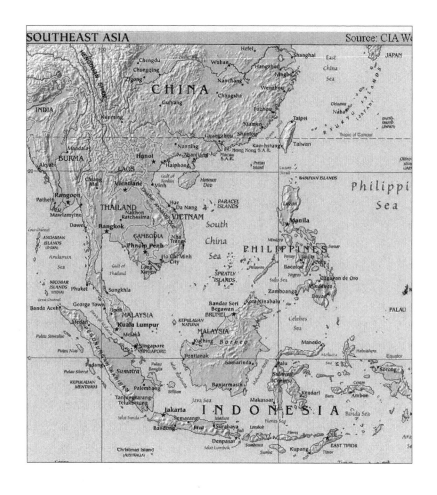

CIA map of Southeast Asia, late 1975 ~
after the fall of Saigon

chicago

October 20, 2015

# *I*MAGINE

Imagine you could turn back the clock, retrace your steps. What part of your past would you choose to relive?

When all your parents' belongings have been distributed and donated, and now you're sorting through what remains— the memorabilia from two long lives—this is where the mind wanders. Or at least mine did.

And then I found the letters.

They were in a manila envelope filled with clippings— articles published, job promotions, awards won, wedding invitations, graduation programs—and among the artifacts of what my parents considered my lifetime milestones were all the tri-folded, blue parchment Par Avion mailers I'd sent home decades ago from the Overland Trail.

They recalled another time and place, where the living was slow and easy, hot and spicy, sexy and funny; a journey that permanently altered my world view and self-perception, a memory that has kept me forever young.

THOUSANDS OF ADVENTURERS took that same journey in the 1960s and 70s, traveling overland from London to Bali in the footsteps of Marco Polo, in search of enlightenment, cheap drugs and free love.

It was an impulse. I was 24. Two years out of college, the protest movement and a short-lived marriage, I quit my job and booked a one-way flight to Tokyo to visit family friends on diplomatic assignment who'd invited my parents and gotten me instead.

The thought of depleting my savings and traipsing off to Asia had never occurred to me. While my friends were doing Europe on $5 a day I had stayed home, angling for a promotion out of my entry-level media job. I was a plotter, a planner, a maker of lists. I'd never met a yellow-ruled pad I didn't like, a competition I didn't feel compelled to win. Go with the flow? No.

But once the idea struck it was a *fait accompli*. A few weeks later, a dour Japanese customs official was stamping my brand-new passport at Tokyo Haneda Airport.

I spent a whirlwind, fascinating month at the embassy, then moved along to Hong Kong. There I checked into the Kowloon YMCA, bought an adorable, gilt-edged, pocket atlas at a flea market and perused it on the rooftop deck overlooking the harbor, all atwinkle from the lights of the junks and ferries transporting wealthy Britons to their homes on Victoria Peak.

No element of this scene could be reproduced today. The Brits have lost their lease, the Y has been torn down and no way could I read such tiny type in that dim light.

According to my baby atlas, Bali was due south of here, 8 degrees below the equator. *Bali Hai.*

I turn some wee pages. Thailand. *The King and I.* Cool.

That was it. Decision made, research concluded, both choices heavily informed by my love of Rodgers and Hammerstein, I returned to my room and had a massive panic attack. I stayed up all night, filling pages of my journal with anxiety and self-doubt, until finally, sick of my own sniveling, I straightened up and marched forth to circle the globe with my guitar over my shoulder and my head up my ass.

# bali

### November 23, 1975

**Immersion.**

Men in skirts, screaming in my face: You! Mister!
YOU! MISTER! WHERE YOU GO?

I'm dragging my suitcase towards customs where right
away I'm busted for leaving a question on the embarkation
card blank.

The official taps the empty space: *REASON FOR VISIT.*

These existential questions—*WHERE YOU GO?* and
*WHY YOU GO?* I will no doubt ponder in the coming months.
But right now, I have no answer so succinct as to fit in this
tiny little square.

"Just write '*business*' or '*personal*,'" says the Aussie
behind me. "Yanks!" he snaps, like men say, *women!*

*Personal*, I write. "Where's the currency exchange?"

Customs Guy stamps my pristine passport with a flourish. "No Ingrish. No change money." He gestures helpfully at the shuttered currency exchange window, chalks an X on my guitar case and waves me onward to figure out where I'm going, how I'm going to get there and what I'm going to use for cash.

Outside the terminal, the city of Denpasar has turned out to greet the arrivals deplaning from Pan Am flight 812.

It's past midnight at the height of monsoon season, and the streets are jammed. Women display sundries on blankets spread across muddy ground, surrounded by fruit peels, snack wrappers, and children up way past bedtime. Men flail their arms, wave signs, passengers snake through the crowd in attempt to avoid them, choking exhaust fumes mingle with a kind of coconutty aroma: Bali.

"Hey you! Mister!"

The humidity is dense, cloying; you can smell it, taste it, feel it in your bones.

"YOU! MISTER!" Someone's planted in my path, shouting at me while I'm gasping like a suffocating fish.

A kid steps between us and nudges him aside.

"Hi, Mister Lady," he says in normal conversational tones. "Where you go? Kuta Beach? Where you stay? I got nice place for you."

The beach part sounds good, the stab at a correct gender reference wins me over; besides, I don't have a lot of options. So I entrust my fate to a teenager in a sarong and a Batman tee-shirt.

He weaves us through the melee, balancing on his head my impractical suitcase stuffed with inappropriate attire, and leads me to an open pickup with pull-down bench seating.

"Take this *bemo. Dharma Yuda*," he tells the driver.

"Does he take travel checks?"

The driver hurls my bag onto the truck. "No trapel check." We lurch through the pitch dark streets of Denpasar,

4

Bali on roads that go from bad to worse to the town of Kuta Beach, where the pavement ends.

The roosters are crowing by the time he slams on the brakes in front of a single-story stucco building. "DHARMA YUDA!" The driver grabs my bag and pounds on the door, rousing an office clerk.

"Yank," the driver says. "Trapel check."

"No trapel check," says the clerk. "Private room, *way-say*. Breakfast. Twelve-hundred." He indicates a damp sign peeling off the wall. The exchange rate is 400 rupiah to one US dollar.

"THREE DOLLARS!"

"Private room! *Way-say*," he protests, by way of justifying the high price. "*Passaporte!*" He pushes the hotel registry across the counter for me to sign: name, country of origin, passport number.

I turn to the driver. I'm not going to be able to pay him. But he's already gone.

"Follow me," says the clerk. I trot after him through a lushly planted courtyard. "I didn't pay that guy."

He strides to the veranda and up a few stairs, pushes a door open and hands me the key. "He be back. Here you room. Best in house!" He points to a doorway on the opposite wall. "There. *Way-say*. Breakfast until 9 o'clock."

It's a nice-sized room, with a double bed, and tall, mirrored teak armoire. Armies of workaholic ants are building colonies on the freshly mopped terra cotta tile floor. There's a bedside table, a life-saving overhead fan, a straw mat ceiling. The bathroom—*so that's what he was saying, W.C.*—is lit and ventilated through a hole in the wall. There's an open drainpipe in the concrete floor with a bucket beside it—calling it a squat toilet would be a stretch—and a dripping shower head that will never turn all the way on or all the way off.

The mattress is OK but the linens stink of mildew. I sprinkle talcum powder on the smelly pillowcase and lie back, not displeased with the turn of events.

I've been deposited, at the pot of gold at the end of the rainbow, at the Eastern end of the Overland, aka 'Hippie' Trail I've never heard of, to start at the finish line. I'm positioned to absorb the collective wisdom of all the travelers who got here the hard way. They hitched and hiked, came on buses and trains, ferries and pickups, all the way from London. Veteran backpackers, many have been away years, not weeks. They've left careers and marriages behind. They'll prove more than willing to show a solo female novice the ropes. I'll be the admiring, respectful protégé, they the wise, all-knowing elders. I'll be taken under a lot of wings.

The first is Sue.

My next-door neighbor, an attractive, chunky blonde on the road with her nine-year-old son, starts mentoring me over breakfast my first day, on the veranda.

"You should order. It comes with the room." I order breakfast, with coffee. She shakes her head. "You like instant? There's only Nescafé over here. Order tea from now on." A column of fire ants are marching towards a streak of egg yolk on her plate. She's unfazed.

"Never trust Aussie men." She spreads marmalade on a piece of white bread and wipes the yolk with it. "They all look like Robert Redford, but they're assholes. I love your accent," she says, mouth full. "It's great to talk to someone from back home."

"What part of the States are you from?"

"Canada." She and her boy had joined the Overland Trail by way of the USSR. This is unusual, but so is traveling with a school-age child.

In the afternoon, in a torrential downpour, Sue guides me to a café in town that accepts travel checks.

The patrons—all sullen Robert Redford lookalikes— sit smoking silently. Only one couple converses.

He's a Teddy Roosevelt lookalike: portly, in belted khaki shorts, wool knee socks and hiking boots, wire rim glasses and a mustache. She's in a flowing mu'u- mu'u, with her hair in a bun.

"Tricia!" Sue yells. "Trevor!"

They're Brit teachers on sabbatical she'd met in Perth. We join them and order *es telers*—a blend of coconut pulp, mashed tropical fruit, condensed milk and crushed ice, delicious. And then the ice comes back to haunt you.

"Don't change too much money here," Trevor advises. "You can get 417 to the dollar at the bank in Denpasar."

They're headed north for Ubud, to see the sacred monkey gardens and take in some dance recitals. They're not beach people. They hate sand.

They leave when the rain lets up. "Till we meet again." Tricia has a firm, earnest handshake. "And we shall, you may depend. The Overland Trail is one big small town."

Newly flush with fistfuls of limp, colorful, play money I shop for sundries. Apparently the Third World is where obsolete American merchandise comes to die. Pepsodent toothpaste in aluminum tubes, little packets of Rinso for scrubbing clothes in a cold-water washtub, Palmolive soap in waxed-paper wrapping, long off the market in the US. Its scent transports me to early childhood, my brother handing me a bar: *I dare you to lick this.*

Individual, unfiltered clove cigarettes are sold from a cup beside the cash register, a bargain at ten rupes apiece. Tightly packed and long-burning, they crackle when inhaled and can be set aside and re-lit throughout the day. Their agreeable aroma somewhat masks the pervasive stench of mildew that hovers everywhere.

Puffing on one contentedly I head west along the beach road to take in my first Pacific sunset.

Low on the horizon, a magnificent red sun has burned through the clouds, setting the sky and sea ablaze in pink and orange as it sinks, a fiery semicircle descending into the glowing sea.

It's exquisite. I'm in awe. At first. But then frantic. Darkness has fallen instantly, like a light being switched off. That's how it works at the equator. Day, then night. No dusk. Also no street lights, no familiar landmarks. I have no idea how to get back.

Stumbling along the rutted road I believe to have brought me here I force myself to place one foot in front of the other, breathe normally, and recite the litany from Dune. *Fear is the mind killer.* Is this the way back to the Dharma Yuda? *Fear is the little-death that brings total obliteration.* Sundown sounds: frogs croaking, ducks quacking, birds twittering. *I will face my fear.* Roosters crowing, motorcycles backfiring, monkeys shrieking: *I will permit it to pass over me and through me.* Hey Mister! Where you go?

The next day I pay triple the going rate for a flashlight, and Sue and her son are gone.

IN THE TROPICS it's a constant battle against the humidity, and the Dharma Yuda is losing.

A building of single-story pastel stucco, boasting shabby rooms and unappetizing breakfasts, it's classified as a *losmen*, comparable to a European *pensione*. That got bombed in WWII. But it's well-located, on the beach road close to town, so it attracts a constantly changing cast of short-term tenants who take tea together on the veranda.

One afternoon I join a middle-aged Javanese couple on holiday. The Mrs. speaks a little English and begins coaching me in Indonesia's official language, Bahasa. How to count, key survival phrases: Good morning, thank you and you're welcome, how much, too expensive, where's the bathroom?

"*Terima kasih*," she says. "Sank you."

I write this in my college-ruled notebook and parrot it back to her in monotone. I hardly attempted Japanese, but Bahasa uses our same alphabet, and the words are multisyllabic, distinguishable to the Western ear. With this language I'll have a fighting chance.

Or not. She frowns. *"Terima kasih,"* she repeats in sing-song, bobbing her head.

Bahasa is not a tonal language per se, but it has a lilting, musical quality like Italian, and bobbing one's head while speaking is a sign of courtesy.

"Ter-imah ka-sih," I mimic the pitch change and head bob.

Satisfied, she moves on: *"MAHAL!"* Too expensive!

She asks my age, where I'm from, who I'm traveling with. When I tell her no one, she clutches her breast. "Alone! Not husband, not brother! Oh! You mother so frighten!"

Having seen me off to the armed-guarded security of the Israeli embassy in Tokyo, my mother will get wind of this detour weeks later, when the first tri-folded mailer arrives Par Avion. If she is so frighten, or has other concerns, I'll have no way of knowing.

Our lesson attracts the attention of the Dharma Yuda's latest arrival. Not the typical backpacker, John is in his mid- 40s, lean, blond and divorced, with a 19-year-old daughter in college. He's traveling on the proceeds from the sale of an Arthur Murray dance studio in hometown Kansas City.

He takes over showing me the ropes. We eat street cart satay smothered in onions and a fiery peanut sauce served on a steamed banana leaf.

We buy a gram of hash off some Dutch guy, explore some Hindu temples, attend a traditional Balinese dance recital, hit the open air market. I buy a Zippo lighter and corncob pipe, mosquito coils, some hideous rubber sandals made from recycled tires and several bolts of batik.

I start wearing sarongs, knotting them halter-style like my *Yiddische* foremothers draping themselves in sheets for a *shvitz* in the bath house. The knee-length batiks are cool, affording protection from alternating blasts of sun and the constant, head-to-toe scrutiny of Balinese men.

At night when the rain stops we sit on the veranda and watch the glowing tips of the mosquito coils turn to ash while I fiddle with my transistor radio, trying to tune in the BBC.

One day John motorcycles up north to hang out with the Dutch hash dealer and I rent what the Aussies call a "push" bike. It's old and lumbering, with a crooked pedal, coaster brakes and knobby tires that make for slow but steady going over hard-packed sand, or muddy dirt roads chickens are constantly crossing—they actually do that—and why? This age-old question I am now qualified to address: because they fuckin' feel like it.

Bali has a rooster problem. Too many cocks and not enough hens. The boys are feeling the strain. All day long they crow, not just at sunrise, strutting along the roadsides, sharing their discontent with everyone.

"Why'nt ya shut up," I tell one who's always pecking around the Dharma Yuda, damn sick of his doodle-doing by now. He turns on me with a malevolent screech.

"*Vy* don't you get *oud*? Go to ah SO-shull function." Whose bit is this again? Nichols and May? The 2000-year-old man? Those records crack me up.

"What'd you say?" Nurse Betsy, my new next-door neighbor, has overheard me speaking to a rooster in a Yiddish accent. Fortunately I don't embarrass easily.

"Never mind." I flop into a deck chair. "Have you seen John?"

Three Aussie RNs from Melbourne now occupy Sue's room. There's Betsy, a great-looking blonde, her best friend Anne, a cute brunette, and brown-haired 'country girl' Coralee—Anne and Betsy's description—a co-worker on her first trip abroad who's being shown around by these two more worldly types.

"John went down the frog and toad," Anne answers.

"For a pig's ear," Betsy says.

I look from one to the other, blank.

"He went down the road for a beer," Coralee says. "Can you hear it now?"

"Hear what?" They've been teaching me Aussie slang, words and phrases. For example, I've learned that "pissed" means "drunk," but life is too short to try and pick up on this rhyming thing they do.

Just then John pulls up on the motorcycle and dismounts in a snit, glasses fogged up, soaked clothes clinging to his wiry frame. The trip up north didn't go well. "I ATE SHIT OUT THERE!" The Dutch guy had never showed, and John got stuck riding all the way back over potholed, muddy roads in a cloudburst that had thus far spared Kuta Beach.

"Wow, that sucks." I stifle a giggle. With his hair plastered down, his ears stick out. He looks elfin.

He collapses in a rattan chair. "FUCK!" He cleans his wire-rims on the tail of the wringing-wet white dress shirt he always wears because they're cooler and dry faster than tee shirts, peers through the lenses and pushes his wet hair straight back. "I'm starving. Let's go eat."

I look from John, to the nurses, to a couple of Indonesian college boys on holiday from Jakarta who are eavesdropping nearby. "Okay. You all coming?"

The downpour hits on the way, flooding the streets, flowing into the ditches: *I shoulda peed before we left.* It's slow going. Someone loses a rubber sandal to the muck every so often, bends down to dislodge it, then runs to catch up. Drenched, we stagger into a café on the main drag. The owner has decent English and a knack for sizing up prospects. He zeroes in on me.

"Hi Mister. You here for mushroom?" He points to the chalkboard menu. Blue Meanie omelettes are the daily special. "Good mushroom today. *Very* trippy. Last night, lot of rain. This morning, lot of sun! *Bagus sekali!* They grow right up from the... how you say? Cow shit."

11

"Magic Mushrooms." John wipes his glasses. "I guess he means psilocybin."

I never dropped acid in college, opting to avoid LSD's teeth-grinding crash-landings and rumored chromosome damage, but the mushrooms supposedly produce an intense hallucinogenic experience with none of these crappy chemical side effects.

"Cow shit?" This has a nice organic ring. "Let's do it!"

The college boys need no convincing, but the nurses seem reticent. Anne asks what it feels like.

"Like pot, I guess, only better?"

"We've never tried pot." Anne looks at Betsy. Coralee inspects her fingernails.

"Sure," John says. "What the hell."

The nurses decide they're on board and pretty soon we're tucking into a Magic Mushroom pizza that tastes agreeably similar to a Chicago-style deep dish. Everyone's enjoying it except John. He chews, shudders, forces himself to swallow. Another bite, sip of sickening soft drink, grimace. He shovels another mouthful down, then gags. The rest of us politely avert our eyes.

"Did anyone notice if there was a bathroom in here?" I look at the boys. "*Way-say?*"

They smile beatifically and shrug. *No way-say*, they say.

No hens, no public toilets, no coffee. What gives? And now it's raining on us again. "DAMMIT! Does it even have to rain INSIDE?"

"It's not raining," an Aussie nurse says, then giggles. "And we're not really inside," another says. She spreads her arms wide. "You see? No walls. In point of fact, we are on a *covered patio.*"

Everyone nods: this is deep.

She gestures to the ceiling of palm leaves. "You see?"

I see. "They're beautiful."

The ceiling fronds have become fans held by Balinese dancers, floating above us, dipping and swaying gracefully in time to distant music.

"Who?"

"The dancing ladies." I gesture overhead, comet-like trails of light following my hands. "Wow. Did you see that?"

"What dancing ladies?" A voice says.

I point above, where the ladies were dancing. They're gone. But..."Hey look! The ceiling is breathing."

With this John retches, casts his rattan chair aside and bolts, hand over his mouth. All our heads turn to watch him go.

"Bummer." I try not to giggle. "It's all my fault."

The nurses are howling, pounding the table. The boys reach for his plate.

I find John doubled over out back, heaving into a ditch and grab his waist to keep him from pitching headlong into puke. I mean, what are friends for? "You OK?"

Finally he straightens up. "This is not the drug for me." We watch his last couple meals float downstream. "When the body says no-ooo...." He shakes his head, wipes his mouth with the back of his hand. "I could use a beer."

"Okay, but I HAVE GOT to find..."

"Poppie's has an outhouse." A disco where back-packers, ritzy-hotel guests and Balinese men on the make all mingle, Poppie's is the place to see and be seen on Kuta Beach.

John finds us some seats as I waddle to the outhouse, legs pressed together. I throw the plywood door open, frantically bolt the latch and turn towards salvation—a hole in the floor...which is undulating. It's alive! MAGGOTS! Hundreds of them, inching across the damp concrete. I fling the door open, shrieking hysterically, and race up to John, who's surrounded by Balinese teens, tapping out a percussion solo on the bar, rocking his shoulders to a mambo beat.

13

"These guys are really digging on these Cuban rhythms." At last he's having a good time today. Then he picks up on my vibe. "Whoa! Whatsamatter?"

"The BATHROOM FLOOR! It's covered in fuckin'—hundreds of—I don't know—*maggots* or something!"

He goes to check and comes back, all chivalrous and reassuring. "Honey. There's no maggots. It's the mushrooms." I consider this. The maggots were glowing, neon blue and a sort of mauve, and maybe they don't come in these colors. Still, nothing will induce me to re-enter that W.C. and no way am I walking back alone, so I'm forced to wait while John raps to his fans about his days playing in a conga band in 50s pre-Castro Havana and Bali boys slide into the empty seat beside me, one by one.

"Hey mister," they each say. "Where you from?"

"No English. *Ich spreche Deutsch.*"

"Huh?"

"*DEUTSCH!*" I bark, my four years of study finally paying off. "*Ich bin ein Berliner.*"

The German ruse mostly works, except on one kid, who persists. "What your name? Where you from? Why can't I understand you?"

There's nothing flattering about all this attention, as it bears no relation to how attractive I may or may not be. I'm a foreign woman, an object of curiosity; *but be fair,* says the little voice. *Isn't that exactly what they are to you?*

Another Balinese guy sits down. He's older, more confident.

"No English," I tell him. "*Ich bin Deutsch.*"

"You're German," he says. "And you don't speak English?" He crosses his arms.

"I don't believe you. Any German who's traveled this far abroad can speak English."

This is true, of course. Almost all the Europeans on the Overland Trail speak English fluently.

He watches me comprehend what he's just said.

"All right. You could just say you're not interested."

After he's out of earshot I shake John's shoulder.

"Could we please, PLEASE go?"

John gallantly agrees to escort me.

We set off in a warm, steady rain, storm runoff coursing through the street. The sound is torment, resistance futile. I'm wearing a bathing suit under a sarong. Suppose I were to succumb—*surrender, inevitable; warm pee coursing down my leg, relief, exquisite*—who would ever be the wiser?

We're almost back when the rain lets up, just in time for the parade I hear coming up the street.

"It's getting close! Let's go watch the parade!" "Honey," John says. "There's no parade." "Can't you hear it? Listen."

Sound is surging all around us, like waves you could run your hands over. Frogs croaking, ducks quacking, primates howling from the palms, wild pigs snuffling along the beach road, backpackers out looking for cheap thrills; a cacophony of languages, whiffs of sweat and mildew, coconuts and cloves: Bali.

Back at the Dharma Yuda the ants have established a thriving civilization on the tile floor. Someone's watching from the armoire mirror. *Careful where you step,* she says. She bears no resemblance to the viola-playing, corrective-shoe wearing dork of childhood recollection. This is some beach party girl on an extreme bender. This girl is sunburned, covered in mosquito bites, her hair growing wild from the remnants of a shag haircut. A clove cigarette dangles from her lips. I like what I see.

AT THE ENTRANCE TO THE FLOATING TEMPLE, a crowd is gathered around a man and his python. It coils menacingly around him as everyone grimaces in repulsion and fascination. The Balinese have a thing for reptiles.

Supposedly giant serpents guard the entrance to Tanah Lot, the famous offshore 15th century shrine we've come to see, but no one's up for wading through the incoming tide to find out, so we content ourselves with strolling through the souvenir stands on the beach, where the trinkets and papaya slices and guided tours are being sold.

An adorable little pixie notices me taking pictures and poses for me. One hand on hip and the other balancing a tray of seashells, she flashes a cute, practiced smile with much more poise than you'd expect from a four-year-old, while I, with much less sense than you'd expect from a 24-year-old, don't realize I'm supposed to pay her.

Later in life, I will make amends to this little girl by pressing pesos into the hands of street urchins all throughout Latin America.

The morning after the mushrooms I'm tagging along with the Three Aussie Nurses, riding two-by-two on rented motorcycles up the coast, to venture outside our cut-rate paradise through the villages and rice paddies and roadside temples of Bali.

Thousands of shrines dot this tiny island. The Balinese are Hindu, into ancestor worship and the spirit world, deeply religious. Two ornate pillars carved with swastikas and gargoyles signify a place of worship; they pop up everywhere, out in the open, for everybody's use as the impulse to worship strikes them.

The swastika, I've learned, dates back millennia. Sacred to Hindus, it symbolizes the exact opposite of what it does me: eternal life, good fortune, prosperity.


The villagers congregate to watch us drive by. Naked children scamper around their beautiful, smiling mothers, all carrying babies in batik slings draped across their bare tops. The women hang around together with their broods, always happy to pose for the camera and wave, seemingly without a care in the world.

They live in small shacks made of enormous dried palm fronds nailed onto rough lumber, alongside drainage ditches where they wash their clothes, bathe and cook. Bathrooms are holes dug outdoors, a few feet back from the water supply. They collect rainwater to drink. Roosters strut around each property. The cows wander and pigs meander among the ubiquitous herds of ducks. The older boys tend the ducks and climb coconut trees to bring the fruit down. The older girls watch the younger kids, and all day Father performs backbreaking manual labor in the rice paddy, with the help of a buffalo or an ox if the family is more well-to-do.

Surrounded by the modern world driving past them every day, they continue to live the life subsistence farmers always have, in what appears to be extreme poverty and total bliss. I'll learn the Balinese enjoy a relatively high standard of living. This island produces enough to support them. Their neighbors in Java and Sumatra do not fare as well. There would be no more smiling and waving to white women taking pictures from the backs of motorcycles.

Back within the Dharma Yuda's shabby confines we take stock. Further north, we've heard, people are paying less for rooms no crappier than ours.

"Have you heard about Kayu Aya?" Betsy asks.

It's an Aussie urban legend, a Sydney investor's dream gone bust. He'd built stone villas, with oceanfront decks, showers and flush toilets. Then hard times hit. The electric wasn't wired and construction stopped. Now cattle are grazing the grounds.

Long on ambiance but short on necessities, the villas rent cheap. With Coralee and me bunking together I reduce my daily out-of-pocket by 200 rupiah.

We watch the sun sink into the South Pacific from our deck that first night, mightily pleased with the upgrade in our lodgings.

The girls pick up where Sue left off, warning me off Aussie men.

"As far as they're concerned it's still the 1950s." Betsy lights a gas lantern.

"They just don't know how to talk to women." Anne swats a mosquito. "They're only interested in one thing. They're a bunch of Male Chauvinist Pigs."

"They stand around all night at the pub talking to their mates." Coralee reaches for a hit from my corncob pipe. "Then right after last call, they walk up and ask to see you home."

The other two nod; standard operating procedure.

"Your guys are different," says Anne. They perceive American men as more considerate, sensitive, enlightened; interested in girls as people, not just sex objects.

This is no mere perception. The American guys I meet on this trek will live up to this reputation, almost to a man. Right on, my Yank brothers.

The girls take day-trips on the scooters into the mountainous interior while I'm felled by a virulent outbreak of Bali Belly. I idle for days on the oceanfront deck, strumming the guitar, sipping tea and searching for radio reception.

On Saturday night I strike gold. The Far East Network comes in: Armed Forces Radio. Waves lapping at the shore, the frogs and crickets chirping, and now some crackle and hiss, and a jangly guitar riff, and John Lee Hooker, he's wailing, 'cause his sugar mama, she ain't sweet no more. Then the velvet tones of a mature black American.

"You're listening to... blues through the night."

He keeps on spinning, smoky, 3AM blues for our boys overseas, and I keep on listening, right beside my Yank brothers.

Eventually the girls move on and I return to one of the Dharma Yuda's cheaper rooms, trading the cold shower drip for the tepid communal dip in the traditional *mandi*.

On sunny mornings I bike around, shooting photos. A Balinese boy carrying harvested bundles of rice lashed to a pole across his shoulders flashes me a brilliant smile; a toothless woman balancing an enormous basket on her head scowls; her gums blackened by betel nut; the children always wave and shout: *WHERE YOU GO?*

The rice paddies are a photographer's dream. Palm trees tilt at pleasing angles over the flooded fields, terraced against hillsides, or sloping down to low-lying streams or marshes.

Three growing seasons keep the farmers busy year-round. It's a backbreaking cycle of germinating, planting, tending, harvesting, bringing to market, using age-old tools and techniques. Right now it's the harvest. Families are out in the paddies in peaked sun hats, whacking at the rice with scythes, while I observe, an alien from another time and place.

SHORTLY BEFORE I'M PLANNING TO LEAVE BALI Nurse Coralee comes pedaling back to the Dharma Yuda. Gone are Betsy, Anne, and the motor scooter.

"They've had enough. Gone home."

She brings me up to speed. Passing Kayu Aya, they'd actually *met* the Sydney Investor. There was chemistry with Betsy. Drinks were had, then dinner, more drinks: then the details become discreetly sketchy. Some variation on the old one-thing-led-to-another; her feelings had gotten hurt and she'd flown off in a huff, Anne at her side.

Coralee, however, is game to go on.

We prepare in earnest. We handwash our clothes and hang them to dry, send mail, shop the outdoor market: its rickety stalls on deeply furrowed ground, covered in betel nut shells and fruit peels, where freshly slaughtered ducks hang by their necks, swinging in the breeze.

19

"Mosquito coils, insect repellent, Rinso." Coralee sidesteps some cow dung. "Anything else?"

"I could use a couple more sarongs."

We sort through a pile of batiks, negotiating in Bahasa to show these women we two have been around the block. Somehow they're not impressed. Their prices are high, the fabrics so-so, but then I spot an unusual piece, with whorls of navy blue, black and white in a dramatic, authentic-looking pattern. I love it, have to have it. I drive a hard bargain and get it for half the price of the other pieces. I'm definitely getting the hang of haggling.

Next I make a huge score—a used, bright yellow copy of *Southeast Asia on a Shoestring*—the only Hippie Trail guidebook in existence. No one who has one will trade or sell it.

I stuff everything in my army-surplus daypack, assuming we'll never outpedal the gathering storm.

"Follow me," says Coralee.

She leads us expertly about the turnarounds.

Veering right when my instinct says left, heading straight when I think we should turn, she gets us back right before the late afternoon downpour hits.

Our last day in Bali is sunny and breezy. Under brilliant blue skies I bike through the coconut groves, eat street-stall *satay* slathered in peanut sauce, order my final *es teler*, then spend an idyllic afternoon on Kuta Beach, watching crabs scuttle the sand and surfers ride the waves while the sun sinks into the Pacific, setting the clouds and the water aflame on its way down.

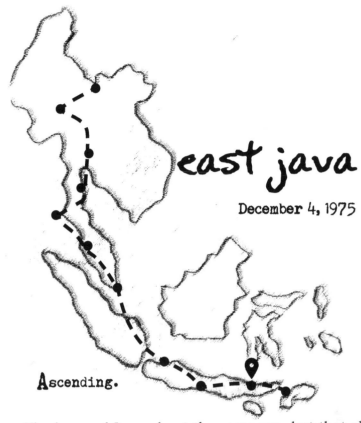

**east java**

December 4, 1975

**A**scending.

The bus and I are about the same age, but that old Blue Bird's got quite a few more miles on her.

We've set out at dawn for Gilimanuk, the port town on the island's northwest tip, where the Strait narrows and ferries cross back and forth all day between Bali and Java.

"Over here." Coralee takes a seat beside a stuck-open window. "This'll let in the breeze. Where's The Book?"

Giddy with the novelty of having printed reference material, we read various uninformative passages to each other as the elderly vehicle gasps and wheezes up the winding coast road, sheet metal banging.

"The ferry only takes about 15 minutes, then we walk to town where we catch a bus to Probolinggo," Coralee says.

"How long's that supposed to take?"

"Doesn't say."

We plan to stop overnight to watch the sunrise over Mount Bromo and its smoking crater the following morning, a sight not to be missed, according to The Book. Though the authors obviously had; they don't know jack about getting to Mount Bromo. Catch a *bemo* to the village near the trailhead, The Book advises.

"What village? Where's the trail head? How long's the hike?"

"Doesn't say."

The bus hits a nasty pothole and a pretty girl behind us starts groaning, leaning forward with head in hands. A few more bumps and she's got the dry heaves.

Noting this in the rearview mirror, the driver pulls over and brings her a coffee can from under his seat. She positions it between her knees, hunched over. She starts retching around the next turn.

"Morning sickness, probably," Nurse Coralee says. "Poor kid."

We gain altitude, passing the mountain villages of the real Bali, where the tourists don't go. We buy fruit through our stuck-open window from the women who always rush out of nowhere to sell food at every stop: oranges or whole pineapples they peel in seconds. Then we're thirsty. In the next village we surrender and buy a bottle of nauseating soda pop through the window. It only makes us thirstier.

"Let's have a fag, get rid of this terrible taste." Coralee lights a clove cigarette. We're passing it back and forth, the seats are bouncing, the windows are rattling; the old Blue Bird, her shocks long dead, is swerving right and left to avoid road ruts when suddenly we slam into a wide, deep gash there's no way around.

The impact jars a window loose and sends shards flying: the sound of shattering, and then a little cry. A jagged piece of glass has sliced an old lady's arm.

In either of our countries this ride would be over now.

Everyone would be screaming, the bus would be emptied, another one radioed for and the trip delayed indefinitely. The injured passenger would be taken to a hospital and everyone else asked to sign damage waivers.

Here, the delay is momentary. The other riders chat and snooze while the driver retrieves the coffee can from the pregnant girl, who hasn't thrown up in a while. He rinses it out at the roadside, mixes ditch water, dirt and sand together to form a paste, then returns and gently inspects the old lady's arm for embedded glass.

Finding none, he slaps the mud on the wound to staunch the bleeding, grips the injured crone's wrist firmly and holds her arm above her head, like something you'd see on a Civil War battlefield. Nurse Coralee looks like she's watching a horror movie.

Presently the old woman's eyes brighten. She manages a toothless smile. The bleeding stops. The driver settles her into her seat, collects the broken glass in some newspaper and off we go.

When her stop comes she gathers up her packages, flashes the driver a gummy grin and pats him on the shoulder, grateful for the excellent customer service.


THE TOWN SQUARE IS DESERTED.

It's getting dark and cold, and we still need to find lodgings and line up a ride to the trail head the next day.

Normally villagers approach travelers, hawking places to stay, but we've arrived after the last scheduled bus and no one is expected this late. Everything's closed, shrouded in mist. My gut is roiling. The Bali Belly has continued to plague me, and landing hungry, thirsty and homeless in this gloomy town sure isn't helping.

"Wish we'd have gotten here in daylight." I pull on my jean jacket.

"We expected we would! The Book said this was an eight-hour trip." We'd been in transit for 12.

"Goddamn that Book."

That's when the cavalry comes over the hill.

"HEY," someone yells from higher up the street. "Hi! When did you get here?"

A couple girls descend a flight of steps to our level. They're dressed in the mish-mash of Eastern/Western clothing that long time travelers adopt: ankle-length sarongs, hiking boots and jean jackets.

The one who called out to us has long, frizzy red braids and freckles. She shakes her head, clucking sympathetically, looks us over, sizes us up. "Why'd you get in so late?"

Our eyes lock in that moment of silent acknowledgment that always passes between Jews who encounter each other in unexpected places. We are rescued.

"We missed our connection. You know of someplace we can stay?"

"There aren't any *losmen* in this town. You have to find someone to take you in." She gestures upward. "We're staying at a *warung* at the foot of the crater. Restaurant owners sometimes take lodgers."

The other girl speaks for the first time. "There's no more room there."

The redhead gives her a look. "They'll *make* room. It's 500 a night."

They lead us up the winding street. Kim, the Jewish girl, says they've been in Java almost a year, studying folk dance. They've also come to view sunrise over Mount Bromo. Their host has arranged for a guided horseback tour. It's safer, she says, plus the money we spend here supports these people, their culture.

"I'm all for that." Our after-hours ride up the mountain: eleven people jammed in an eight-seat minibus. We'd paid five times the local price. The baked good a grocer wouldn't sell me at twice the going rate; he wanted triple.

"But not charging a set price for things like toilet paper and food? That's not fair."

Friend of Kim chuckles. "Oh. Right. *We* don't pay those kind of prices."

The host is a kindly man eager to provide what scant comfort he can.

He warms up some rice and tea on a propane burner. His wife lights a lantern and shows us to the home's common room, behind the *warung*. The whole family sleeps here— kids, grandparents, and a couple young adult males. Two of them will now be spending the night on a bare wood floor, with the outside damp and chill coming through the chinks in the floorboards.

The four of us get creaky rattan beds, just off the floor, topped by thin mattresses stuffed with hay like young Abe Lincoln slept on.

Kim nods at my guitar. "They're asking if you'll play something. Know any Hebrew songs?" She's all about the cultural exchange.

I rub my hands together to warm them, unzip the plaid case and start tuning up.

The kids are bouncing up and down. They get to stay up late. Some foreigners are putting on a show!

Our host lights a gas lantern while Kim and I harmonize in the ancient tongue, drawing from our deep common repertoire of summer camp and youth group numbers. Then the girls dance—Kim has taught her friend some Israeli folk steps—and the family claps along. Looking around the circle of smiling faces, everyone so appreciative, I feel this experience justifies all those terrible hours spent getting here.

When the lamp goes out, the people we've put out of their beds come to sleep beside us on the floor. Apparently I've displaced the old granny, and she's not a well woman. Deep, violent coughs rack her tiny body.

"Oh my God," I stage whisper to Coralee, "I can't let her lie there." I start to get up.

"Lie down," Kim's friend hisses. "You don't second-guess them. That's not right."

Of course it's not. No Trekkie can dispute the Prime Directive which she has unknowingly invoked, which states the Federation must not interfere with the normal development of other planets or impose their values upon them.

So together we lie, awake all night, an old woman fighting for oxygen and a young one, her conscience.


At 4 A.M. we're plodding through the cold mist on tiny horses across an unworldly plane of volcanic sand and powdered lava. Each of us has a boy guide, and mine is shivering.

I peel off my orange windbreaker and pass it to him. He zips it up and ties the hood. Snotty Girl lets it pass. No one speaks. We're in a dark, dense fog that doesn't promote conversation, or bode well for sunrise.

Finally the lead guide speaks. "This name, Sea of Sand." They pull the horses over and point us towards a treacherous incline, about 300 feet of loose rock leading to the rim. From here we're on our own, and on foot. Looks like we'll be getting our hike in after all.

This morning Bromo is subdued. The sulfur smoke stays low, causing none of the nausea The Book cautions of, but dawn's light never pierces the mist. No warm rays illuminating the steam rising from the caldera or spilling across the desolate landscape onto Bromo's sister peaks—no unforgettable vista, only endless grey.

We approach the rim and contemplate the void. Clouds of sulfur hover above the crater, like the devil just opened his door.

Once we circle the creepy crater and take snapshots, there's not much reason to stick around.

Considering all that time and effort to get there you'd think we'd have stayed longer, but I guess summits are really about getting there.

BACK IN CEMORO LAWANG the sun has burned off the fog. The village is appealing in daylight. Fragrant wood smoke rises from the chimneys of its colorful stucco homes. Beyond, among the terraced fields of corn and vegetables, farmers in wool ponchos lead their goats to graze.

This entire tableau, style of dress included, I'll see again in my travels through Central America.

Kim negotiates our fare for the ride back. A gentle smile, a tilt of the head, some words are said, and the same driver who charged Coralee and me 750 apiece last night is taking us at the local rate—150.

Clearly I need to up my haggling game, maybe adopt a more demure, less strident approach. "What'd you say?"

"It's not what you say," says Friend of Kim, in a tone I've had enough of by now. "It's how you say it. You have to know these people, how to talk to them." Like they do.

The minibus blows a tire. Nobody cries out, nobody moves; no two-hour delay. The driver jacks it up with 12 people inside and puts on the spare in the time it takes me to shoot a couple photos of a family walking alongside the road.

"They remind me of Incas."

"Incas," Kim says. "You've been to Peru?"

"No, there's this group of them always playing flutes outside my office."

Friend of Kim smirks, her opinion of me continuing its downward spiral. "You don't just point a camera in people's faces," she says. *Again* with the tone. "This isn't Bali."

"Where do you think you'll be staying in Jogjakarta?" Coralee interjects.

"We haven't decided." She looks at me. "We don't like to travel in groups."

We change buses In Surabaya. Central Java's infamous hub city that attracts sinners of all sorts, where the law is lax and sanitation non-existent. It's a town of general ill repute that sure looks the part.

The depot is a scene of total squalor. Hustlers jostling beggars, horns blaring, people shouting, dogs barking, horses whinnying. The stifling air stinks of exhaust fumes and sewage.

Peddlers block the path of everyone attempting to debark. There's lots of pushing, and lots of attention directed at the four white women lined up to get off the bus.

I freeze on the bottom stair. "Holy crap. I'm not going out there." Everyone behind me is brought up short.

The bus driver starts yelling.

"He's saying you have to get off here," Kim translates. "It's the end of the line."

Coralee peers over my shoulder. "Quite a disgusting shithole," she says, in her proper Aussie diction. "Where's the bus to Jogja?"

The driver shouts something.

"There's one about to leave," Kim says. The two girls exchange meaningful glances. "You better hurry."

"You're not coming?" we chorus.

"We're going to stay for a while, have a look around," says the snotty friend, and gathering their things up without even a 'so long,' they plunge into the swarm of bodies, Kim's red braids swinging side to side.

Soon they're engulfed in the crowd.

28

# jogjakarta

December 6, 1975

**Transition.**

A university town that attracts long-term travelers intent on learning the language and culture, Jogjakarta is nowhere near a beach. It seems quite the metropolis after Kuta Beach and its gravel roads. The streets teem with cycle and foot traffic, horse-drawn carriages and bicycle cabs; peddlers selling from pushcarts, merchants hawking from street stalls.

The energy is a welcome change from the languor of Bali. I love the constant commotion, the incongruity of it all: the oxcarts clattering and jackhammers thundering, the volcanic peaks, minarets and construction cranes looming overhead. It's a city teetering on the cusp of modern times, while retaining the charm of its colonial and more distant past.

29

We book dollar-a-day singles at the Hotel Kota—finally, a decent recommendation from The Book. A once-stately Victorian that housed foreign dignitaries in colonial times, the Kota now rents out spartan single rooms to Overlanders who congregate in the lounge and discuss Products We Miss from Home.

"Nutella on toast," says an Aussie voice outside my room that first morning.

"Vegimite," says another.

"Cheese cake from Sara Lee," says a Yank in reverent tones.

I throw my door open. "Original or cherry topping?"

Among the Kota's various female residents studying some sort of folk art, two are named Ann.

American Ann who loves Sara Lee has short dark hair in ringlets. "We're going to have to send you to our tailor."

Aussie Ann who is perfectly accessorized chimes in. "You can't walk around Jogja in sarongs. This isn't Bali."

Coralee and I take our batiks to the Anns' Chinese seam- stress, who objects to working with such crap. She'll deign to make me three dresses, but my favorite, the blue piece I negotiated the great price for, she won't touch.

"Not use this! SECOND HAND!" She points out a black patch that has been artfully stitched to blend in with the design and tosses it at me. "They trick you."


JOGJA'S ARTSY VIBE gets my creative juices flowing, and my tiny windowless room has great acoustics, with its foot-thick concrete walls and lack of furnishings that muffle sound. I devote hours to writing and singing and playing guitar.

I'd started writing songs in puberty when some boy made me feel bad. Later my musings took on political and philosophical themes. By now I have a couple box sets worth of material nobody's ever heard.

I had always dreamed of fame. Not for me the destiny of my mother's generation, the grocery shopping with the hair in curlers, the PTA meetings. I aspired to be Somebody. First, a Famous Actress, next, a Famous Writer. Then I traded the viola for a guitar. Famous Songwriter. Common denominator: I would be Famous.

So I venture out of my cell into the Kota's lounge and start sprinkling some original stuff in with the covers. And people listen. They listen not only to the music, but the lyrics, and they come up to talk to me about them afterward.

As my singing and playing begin to attract an audience, I start wondering if I could actually pull this off.

The monsoon season is on the wane. The sun shines for long periods during the day now, though conditions still change abruptly in the evening, when torrential downpours move in from the mountains and wreak havoc.

My first Friday night at Helen's café—Overlander headquarters—a ferocious storm hits. Rain barreling down, the proprietor shuttering us in, explosions outside like a bomb going off, the place is in polyglot panic: *Erdbeben! Sous les tables! Jauh dari jendela!* Good Lord, TAKE COVER!

Java is not the place you want to hear thunderous, unidentifiable commotion coming from outdoors. It's the world's seismic hotspot, plagued by every manner of catastrophe: hurricanes, earthquakes, tsunamis.

Although this time the cause is benign. The rain has driven a tin shed aground, and it's clattering like hell on its way down.

Someone bursts through the door, a rugged, rangy type who fills the entryway and even drenched, he's the best-looking man to cross my path in some time. He shrugs off his dripping US Army surplus rain poncho, pushes his wet, dark-blond hair off his forehead, looks around the room, and his eyes come to rest on me.

Bill moves his broad shoulders side to side when he talks, responds expansively to every question and asks few. He's 34, an environmental engineer whose four-year contract with an Australian company has just ended. His face is etched by smile lines earned working outdoors. His eyes are hazel, mischievous, confident. "See you home?"

Back at the Kota a group has gathered in the main lounge.

"Hey Chicago," someone yells. "You gonna play tonight?"

"What do you play?" Bill's tone is pleasingly flirty.

He comes to my tiny windowless room where I switch on the bare 40-watt bulb and grab my guitar, with its mess of excess steel string protruding from each peg.

"What's this, a Dylan thing?"

"No, I hate it, but when I restrung it I didn't have a wire cutter."

"I can clip those for you, nice and neat. I have pliers back in my room."

"You travel with pliers?" I flirt back.

"I need 'em to mind my gear."

"Mind my gear," I repeat. "You sound like an Aussie."

He shrugs, closing my door behind us. "Four years in their country."

I finish my set with a Stones' ballad, watching Bill watching me. *I've got no expectations to pass through here again*; neither does he.

The audience gives me a nice hand and Bill approaches my little stage, swinging those long legs, deliberate and confident and slow. "Coming with me?"

Yes I am.

"Rain's starting again. Do you have something to put on?"

I throw the orange windbreaker over my purple tie-dyed Indian cotton dress. It's a hideous combination, but it's dark out, and raining. Who cares?

Bill cares. "You're going to wear THAT?" This is not a question I'd have expected from someone in a fishing vest.

Through rainy streets to his room: private entrance.

High ceilings, tall screened windows, a ceiling fan twirls. There's a table and chairs, a double bed. A far cry from my room at the Kota.

He lights a couple gas lanterns and starts rummaging through his equipment in search of his prize possession—an antique compass in a leather case. "Know how to use one of these?" He rotates it in his hand. "Not sure where this'll take me next. Stay here? Tour around? I dunno. After four years of knowin' exactly where I have to be each day it's nice to just go with the flow."

He clips my guitar strings, nice and neat, then offers me a hit of Buddha, potent, and a drink of water from a canteen, bitter.

"Taste the iodine? I'm used to it." The rain picks up. "Boy, it's really coming down now. Guess you're going to have to stay here." He smiles and pats the bed next to him.

I bide my time, we talk some more, then he extends a hand, palm up. "C'mere."

On the bed he enfolds me in his arms, rests my head against his chest and strokes my hair. He rocks us gently side to side. "I just want to hold you, baby."

We hold each other. We listen to the rain some more, each other's breathing. I look up from his shoulder, he leans down, the curtains drift, the lanterns flicker.

A long while later, after the rain has stopped, Bill steps back into his underwear and blows out the lanterns. We sleep very well together.

Over the weekend he drops out of sight. The flow seems to have taken him elsewhere. At home I might have expected a phone call, here on the road, there are no phones and no expectations.

Still, what our night together lacked in substance it made up for in form. So sensual, so romantic! Eyes meeting across a crowded room, lanterns flickering, rain falling. *I just want to hold you, baby.* I'm gonna get a great song out of this.

MONDAY MORNING I'm writing at my favorite table when some-one interrupts my train of thought.

"Excuse me. HELLO? Have you seen Ann?"

"American or Australian?"

"American. We're going for *nasi padang* tonight."

"Uh-huh. She'll be around later." I resume writing.

He walks over and stands there till I look up to discover I'm being scrutinized by a short, slight, cute, auburn-haired, unmistakable New York Jew.

"Hi. I'm Cliff." He turns a chair backward and sits. "Ever try Padang food?"

That night he organizes a group from the Kota to experience Sumatra's native cuisine.

We're seated communally at long tables already laden with many bowls of unappetizing, unidentifiable foodstuffs.

"Forks and spoons," Cliff says. "Not completely authentic. In Sumatra we'd be eating with our hands."

I reach for the only familiar-looking item, a hard-boiled egg with the comforting purplish hue of a potato that's been dunked in beet borscht.

Cliff's warning look comes too late. I have bitten into the hard-boiled egg from hell: punishingly hot, sour and rancid, the most disgusting flavor combination I have ever encountered.

"RICE!" he yells. There aren't any napkins, so I spit fiery egg in my hand, which burns on contact. "Here." He hands me a Kleenex. My nose is running. "Don't touch your eyes."

Over the next few days Cliff plans enriching day trips in the area. Shame I didn't like the Padang food, he says. Eaten regularly, the spice wards off mosquitoes, also killing certain digestive bacteria. He's an expert on this topic, having taken ill in Nepal. "You've heard of Freak Alley?"

"In Kathmandu?" It's the legendary back-packer district, where Overlanders smoke hash and talk about trekking the Himalayas.

"Right. Dirtiest place I've ever seen. Worse than India."

He'd woken up in a British hospital, not remembering how he got there. He'd been kept there nine days and dropped 21 pounds he couldn't afford to lose.

"The doctor said, 'Good heavens, man! We thought you were a goner.' Watch it, loose rocks." He's sure-footedly climbing a crumbling wall at Taman Sari, a ruined retreat a sultan built for his concubines in the 1700s. "Not much to see. Great view from up here, though."

I take some photos of Jogja's tile roofs and rainy season lush greenery.

"Snapshots." He shakes his head. "You need an SLR when it's this overcast."

I don't know what an SLR is and keep taking my snapshots.

Cliff is 33, a lapsed attorney who'd made partner in record time, then become disenchanted with the profession and the emptiness of the materialistic, acquisitive life he and his first wife were leading in Scarsdale.

"Don't buy that." He takes a cute item from me, a *becak* driver pulling his fares in a bicycle cab. "Cheap crap. Look, you can bend it."

"So there's a *second* wife?"

"Tellya later." Right now he's trolling the goods. Cliff does what most backpackers only talk about: he earns a living on the road. He scouts markets for fabrics and folk-artsy objects, then ships them to his business partner for distribution in Southern California, where he moved after his divorce.

I gather up some serving spoons and figurines.

"I just want some cheap little *tsotchkes* to send home. This is all I can spend."

"Uh-huh. Or how about some batik? Jogja is known for its batik."

"I already bought some in Denpasar."

"That's the *worst* possible place to buy batik. They palm second-hand material off on tourists who don't know any better. Aw jeez, lookit this. Pathetic. HEY!"

He approaches a bleary-eyed woman selling fruit. Her tongue and lips are black, and she's surrounded by empty shells. "Betel nuts. Ever try 'em? No? Good. A highly addictive carcinogen. Like in South Pacific? *Bloody Mary's chewin' betel nuts*," he sings. "That's gonna kill ya," he tells the woman. "*Tidak makan ini!*"

"*Pergi neraka.*"

"Bitch."

I tell Cliff how influential this show tune had been in my deciding to come here.

"*Bali Hai, will call you...*"

"Actually," he says, "Bali Hai is in the New Hebrides."

So. I flew to the wrong island. An honest mistake. That I based my entire trip on. Guess I should've done my homework.

Suddenly lots of squealing erupts from a yellow school bus inching through the horse-and-buggy and bicycle traffic. A uniformed schoolgirl is pointing at us.

"Dustin Hoffman!" She shrieks. "Barbra Streisand!"

We crack up. Cliff gets this a lot.

"When I first started traveling, this guy told me I looked like 'The Graduate.' 'Oh, sure, I say. Dustin Hoffman.' Then, after I'd been on the road a while, this other guy says, 'You look like that actor—what's his name again?'

'Dustin Hoffman,' I say, 'from The Graduate.' And he goes, 'no not him. The guy who was in Midnight Cowboy.'"

We both laugh at the punch line.

"Another time, this woman says, 'Excuse me, but... are you the same kind of person as Henry Kissinger?' I'm like, gee, great. Ratso Rizzo. Henry Kissinger."

"I was thinking more George Segal." This is a highly flattering comparison in 1975.

He smiles. "OK, Barbra."

I get an image of Streisand, longing unrequitedly for Robert Redford in his dress whites in *The Way We Were*. An enormous talent, but... "Do I *really* look like her?

"Nah." He leans over and plants a smooch on the tip of my straight, small nose.

On the way back, Cliff says we should stop at a flower stall to bring some back for the room—his room has become *the* room. Presumptuous, but smooth. In fluent Bahasa he negotiates with the flower vendor, buying more each time she drops her price until we have bushels of blooms.

As we stroll back to the Kota arm in arm, passersby glance our way pleasantly and murmur.

"*Menikah*," Cliff repeats. "'Married.' They can't conceive of any male-female relationship outside marriage in this culture."

Interesting. This must be why people treat me nicer when I'm with Cliff. Service is prompt, manner deferential, ogling minimal; at his side I'm legitimized, seen as a properly escorted, respectable woman.

Though guys traveling with girls are also seen as more responsible, less apt to raise hell. They get hassled less at border crossings, questioned and searched less invasively. We're useful to and dependent on each other, in ways we aren't at home. There's lots of incentive to pair off.

Back at the hotel we run into Aussie Ann, lovely as usual in a batik sundress and wooden-beaded necklace. She's the kind of pretty girl who makes anyone standing next to her look like a troll doll, but you really like her anyway, because she gets that her beauty is just a happy accident, not some accomplishment she gets to lord over the rest of us. At the Kota, many a man will try and fail with Aussie Ann.

Cliff marches up and gets her in a lip lock. *So there's some history here?* She shoves him off. *Or not.* She admires my armload of flowers, avoiding him. Did they? Didn't they? One cannot say, and does not ask.

Cliff's deluxe corner room has high ceilings and windows, wall hangings draped behind two double beds, a nightstand, mirror, a desk. He magically produces flower vases from the closet, then starts fuming over a letter from his business partner and firing back a response.

I turn from arranging the flowers. "Carbon paper?"

"You know where I can find a Xerox machine around here?" He gestures out the window as a horse and carriage clatter by. "I keep records of all correspondence with that woman." He sounds so vehement I ask if the relationship is all business.

"STRICTLY platonic." He seems pleased by the question. "Listen to this." Snottily mimicking her voice. "'You've lost sight of our customers' preferences.' What a bitch. 'Find some batiks in cool blues.' Ridiculous. Who buys BLUE batik?"

It's been a long day. "I'm going for a *mandi*." By now I've adopted the Indonesian practice of taking multiple dipper baths per day, lathering up beside the communal concrete washtub and rinsing down with cold water.

"Okay. Come back when you're ready and we'll talk about dinner," he says. Just like we are *menikah*.

In a few days we've become a couple, so typical of the Trail. Relationships that might build over months at home are compressed into days here. Each step in the arc is the same—meeting, discovery of shared interests, mutual attraction, the blossoming of romance; the growing familiarity with each other's quirks—some of which begin to annoy—the divergence of opinion—what next? Here or there? Together or apart? It all still takes place, just at a very accelerated pace.

Yet mailing a letter takes all morning, getting film developed, a week. Everything's opposite here. *Bizarro world.*

I punch on the bare-bulb overhead, flop down on the uncomfortable mattress and fire up a bowl.

Cliff knocks and enters in high spirits. "We're leaving for Bali in the morning!

"Better crumble some tobacco into that pipe. That Buddha grass is really strong."

I take an unadulterated hit. "I'm not going back to Bali."

"You haven't *been* to Bali," he retorts. "You've been to *Kuta Beach.*"

Cliff disapproves of how I'd lazed around Kuta, never seeing the *real* Bali. He can't let it drop. I was a Tourist, not a Traveling Woman, someone of depth and purpose. He so admires these women, loves seeing them lined up on the verandas of low-budget *losmen,* writing letters while their center-parted, just- shampooed hair and hand-washed laundry dry in the sun.

"I made a rule," I say. "No backtracking."

Now he's pissed. A RULE? Of all the stupid reasons not to do something. "That's a very LINEAR mindset. Open up! You're on a journey, not a 'trip.' There's a whole world to experience out there beyond...Michigan Avenue!"

"Michigan Avenue!" Nice zinger there, he hadn't told me he knew Chicago.

"So this is how you act when you don't get your way? All—insulting and condescending?"

Cliff runs his hand through his excellent head of hair and looks up with theatrical flair. "NO. I will not be rejected right now." He crosses his arms. "Not after everything I've just been through."

I'm holding a hit and don't bite, not that I would have.

"When I first saw you, I thought you were about 18 years old. You know why?" He lifts my chin. "You wouldn't make eye contact. Like some teenager."

Eye contact. Teenager. I was writing something, he was interrupting my train of thought. This man is a piece of work. And yet...I'm not asking him to leave. Not that he would. It's show time.

"So. You were wondering about my second wife?"

I lean back against the concrete wall, take another hit and wave goodbye to dinner. "Not really."

39

Cliff spends the next few hours reenacting scenes from his love life: gestures, voices, dialects, poses. The Jewish first wife in Scarsdale; the law firm, rat race and bourgeois lifestyle that had ceased to fulfill him. The WASP second wife, a beautiful blonde whose mother told her Jewish husbands usually cheat but were excellent providers. She'd tired of him, used him as a stepping stone to greener pastures, broken his heart.

Then the California couple he'd met in Acapulco; the husband a suave, debonair Latin American, the wife another blonde ice goddess, the threesomes that continued back in LA. She took Cliff's breath away. He couldn't get her out of his mind.

I shift around on the bed. My ass is falling asleep.

Eventually he'd gone berserk, leaving her after each *ménage à trois* in the arms of her macho stud, and handed her an ultimatum: him or me.

Surprise, surprise, she picked Julio Iglesias over Dustin Hoffman. They apologized for invading his emotional space and left him in psychological tatters.

All this Mid-Seventies Southern CaliforniaSpeak is giving me a headache. I'm starving, I'm thirsty. I've been trapped on a mattress that crunches when I move with my back against the wall, smoking dope and watching *Days of Our Lives* for the last few hours.

"I just can't accept any more disappointments." At last, the closing argument. "Come with me to Bali."

We stare each other down, his gaze steely and determined, mine stubborn and bloodshot, an irresistible force against an immovable object, for an unnatural length of time.

Finally he stands. "All right." His voice softens. "We've shared a great deal of ourselves tonight."

I'd said about six words.

"We're tired. Let's just say good night." And at last, he's gone.

NEXT MORNING, ALL SMILES, he intercepts me emerging from the mandi. "*Selamat pagi!* Parangtritas! We're going for the weekend. It's a beach town, only 28 kilometers away. You'll get to see the Indian Ocean."

"So what's with Bali?" Yesterday he'd had urgent business there that couldn't wait.

He gives a cute, self-deprecating shrug. "I was just trying to sweep you off your feet."

Scenes from the evening replay in my mind. *Linear mindset. Michigan Avenue.* Helluva technique. And yet...I go and get my things.

We travel south to the Opak River, the ancient bus spewing noxious fumes across miles of subsistence plots on volcanic soil that produces the region's distinctive purplish-black rice. I'd seen the harvest in Bali. Now families are back out in the paddies, planting.

Some women board with a herd of ducks, nodding and smiling at us. *Menikah*, they say, little Javanese Yente the Matchmakers commenting on how well-suited we are—and who would disagree? Certainly neither of our families.

Under their approving gaze Cliff decides now is the time for some pillow talk. Graphically, though in normal conversational tones, he begins describing certain plans for later that evening as the ladies look on placidly and I attempt to maintain a normal facial expression.

Pretty soon the languid tropical air and explicit chat get to him. "I have an erection," he announces to a busload of passengers. At this point, I'm mortified.

But one day I'll reflect upon this scene with the wisdom of age and realize what a hoot that was, Cliff talking dirty in front of those old crones.

At the river there's a raft bobbing in the water—planks nailed to some garbage drums—and a guy with a pole.

"*This* is the ferry?" Young Abe Lincoln piloted a raft just like this down the Mississippi in 1828. "When does it leave?"

Cliff sighs. Haven't I gotten it yet? No. specific. time—enunciating each word in a manner that could become annoying over the long haul—"They leave when they fill up. Sit down." He points to a grassy patch along the riverbank. "We could be here an hour."

When enough people to sink the raft have assembled he starts poling us across, through waist-deep muddy eddies to the river's south bank.

On the other side we find a graded gravel path banked by rice paddies, palmettos and tropical scrub that stretches towards the limestone bluffs—the road to town.

The natives clap on their peaked hats against the noonday sun, shoulder their heavy bundles, sling their toddlers in sarongs and leave us to trudge in their tracks.

We pass a farmer planting rice, pushing his plow behind a water buffalo, both of them slogging through the muck.

"Ever walk barefoot through a rice paddy?" Cliff asks invitingly. "No? Good." Trick question. "Don't. Worms get under your toenails, you get infected, and by the time you find out, it's too late. You could lose a foot."

He's full of these worst-case scenarios that illustrate the dire consequences to be suffered by the foolhardy, the inexperienced—people like me.

In town we sign in at the visitor registry: name, country of origin and passport number, as all foreigners are required. This allows local *Immigrasi* and our own state departments to keep tabs on us. But it also helps us keep track of each other. I see One-Night Bill was here earlier this week.

The setting is breathtaking, but accommodations are scarce, basic and found only by asking around.

Cliff stops at a grocery with Chinese lettering above the door. "Rule of thumb. When you have a question no one else can answer, find a Chinese. They'll know. They call 'em the Jews of the East." He taps his temple.

"They got '*saichel*.'" *Sense*. Spoken in Yiddish, this is a supreme compliment.

Millions of Chinese deserted the mainland in 1949. Ambitious and driven, at odds with the ideologies of Marx and Mao and put off by those drab unisex worker outfits, they went into diaspora all over Southeast Asia to become its merchant class, fueling local economies wherever they settle.

Sure enough, the grocer tips us off to a *warung* a few doors from the beach with a couple rooms to rent out back. There we're offered the ocean view room, with a grand, ornately carved teak bed. It's wonderful. Only one thing's missing—a mattress.

"The room with the mattress frees up tomorrow." Cliff gestures to the sheet of plywood dressing the bed. "Is this OK, or do you want to find something else?"

The surf is pounding on a sunny afternoon. We've been in transit six hours. "It's OK. Let's go for a hike."

"Great." He seems surprised.

The terrain is varied, unusual. Volcanic black-sand dunes, the color of dirt, yet pure and silky smooth as the glacial golden sands of the Great Lakes, and vegetation you don't usually see side by side, like banana trees and cactus.

We climb a secluded waterfall cascading down a black limestone rock face. Cool, fresh water swirls around us and spills onto the deserted beach. Dark bluffs, brilliant blue sky, the Indian Ocean pounding the black sand, the birds wading and crabs scuttling in the tidal pools: spectacular.

"I've never seen anything quite like this," Cliff almost whispers, a guy who has seen a lot.

At dinner we meet the couple who got the mattress. He's a wide-eyed Javanese teen, she a pretty, amply-built Aussie Traveling Woman draped in sarongs and a roomy, see-through Indian cotton tunic. Few words pass between them, none of them English; the boy mainly gazes at her.

Cliff initiates conversation—innocuous what-to-do-in-the-area type chat. He tells her about the waterfall, she describes a beautiful private grotto they'd found on a hike.

Cliff casts her a knowing glance, just shy of a leer. "Sounds like a perfect spot for playing naughty games."

She gives a dreamy, Mona Lisa smile and strokes her flowing blonde locks.

When they leave I take him to task. "Naughty games! A perfect stranger. What is WITH you?"

"What's with ME? What's she doing here with that underage boy?" He tsks. "She's got this whole colonial, sexual exploitation thing going on."

"Oh, come off it! Colonial. Can't she just be a chunky girl who doesn't get many dates?"

"He's HALF HER AGE! Let her go find a grown man, not some young kid." No double standards. Boy or girl, the child is below the age of consent. I must say I admire Cliff's attitude, I just wish he'd keep it a little more to himself.

But keeping things to himself is not Cliff's way. Throughout the evening, during a romantic interlude that is peculiarly enhanced by the plywood and continuing over breakfast, he keeps me posted on every errant thought that comes to mind. He critiques our night together in explicit detail, pausing just once. "Where do you put it? I couldn't eat like that."

He's watching me inhale my latest order of rice pudding: black rice bound with sweet cream, tossed with chunks of fresh mango, papaya, pineapple and watermelon, all spritzed with lime juice and sprinkled with fresh ground nutmeg. Dense, chewy, delicious. Deadly.

That afternoon we hike to the area's hot springs, envisioning steaming natural pools and crashing surf.

An attendant shows us to a utility shed with a concrete washtub hooked up to some rusty pipes.

"Is this where we change?"

Cliff twists a spigot, lips taut. "These are the springs."
Smelly water starts spilling into the washtub.

"This? Is IT?"

He stares me down. It's like a contest now, which of us can be the better sport.

"Fine." I climb into the laundry tub, emitting oohs and ahs of pleasure as I settle into the stinking hot water. At least afterwards, my mosquito bites no longer itch.

Dinner more than makes up for the bummer baths. "This guy can COOK!" Cliff says, over the roar of the incoming tide. "But he's no businessman. Plywood, he puts us on."

"Actually? It wasn't that bad."

He lights up. "My favorite part was when..."

"*Oy.* Not at the table."

He smiles and sips his warm beer. "This guy needs a business strategy."

Our host is nearby, dreamily smoking a clove cigarette, oblivious to our presence; a real go-getter.

Cliff spears a chunk of fish. "Know what I'd do?" I don't.

"I'd find someone to sell me another mattress for a down payment, then raise the rate on the room. With the extra income, he pays off the store in no time—with interest!"

He signals the proprietor to join us and outlines the plan in fluid Bahasa, ignoring the man's glazed expression that suggests he's just waiting for Cliff to pause for air.

Finally he does and the man flees.

"Great. You just violated the Prime Directive." The Star Trek reference slides right past him, which I'm willing to overlook as I don't plan to bear his children.

"This is a cash economy. Credit, interest. Down payment. They don't know from any of that."

"If they did, they wouldn't be so susceptible to exploitation by the industrialized West."

"Exploitation? And we just paid to sleep on WOOD?"

45

He brushes this aside, a man accustomed to dazzling himself and others with his brilliance. "That's one on one. I am referring to systematic, institutionalized exploitation on a global scale."

"Uh-huh. Find out if he changed the sheets."

Cliff balls up his napkin. "Don't assume there's sheets."

Sunday night at the Kota, Cliff bustles around with nervous energy, organizing the closet, adding fresh water to the flowers. "I really do have to leave for Bali tomorrow." He takes one more shot. "You coming?"

I try the Mona Lisa smile that had so enchanted the Aussie sex offender's adoring victim.

"All right." He knew I wouldn't. "But I want you to keep this room while you're here. I want to make sure it's available when I come back, and I don't want to take all my stuff on the train. I'll pay up in advance."

I shake my head. No double standards.

"Then leave me whatever you'd have paid for your own room." He hands me a key. "It'll be a final act of love and trust between us." The guy has a flair for the dramatic.

The next morning at the depot, an Aussie girl is creating a scene. The train she wants has stopped running, or maybe never did; the kind of thing you just learn to accept. But she hasn't yet. "Where is the student travel office?" she cries. "I'll book it through them."

"That office has shut down," says a lanky Yank in a fishing vest. "Well hey there!" One-Night Bill exclaims, without a trace of embarrassment. "You still around? How's it goin?"

"Great. We just got back from Parangtritas."

He doesn't touch that, just glances at Cliff, then rivets his attention on the flustered Aussie girl in the spikey heels, skin-tight black jeans and studded denim vest.

She totters over to point out a passage in The Book with an acrylic fingernail, bangle bracelets jangling.

"This says the student travel office in Jogja is open weekdays till 5 o'clock."

"Not anymore." Bill gives her the teasing smile that had so recently worked its magic on me.

"That Book was obsolete by the time it went to press," Cliff snaps. He hates The Book. He feels people should rely on their own ingenuity to get around. "You want to know how to get someplace, you ask the people who just came from there." He nods at Bill, then looks her up and down.

"My, that's quite a travel outfit." He has taken an immediate dislike to her.

On Bill, however, she's having the opposite effect. He lasers in on her, looking down bemusedly. "Now just where is it you're trying to get to?"

Back out on the dusty street that runs muddy in the rain, Cliff says, "Spike heels on these streets. Ridiculous. Everything on that woman was artificial."

Exactly. No orange windbreaker. So Bill likes his girls flashy. "Not a Traveling Woman," I agree.

When the whistle blows Cliff kisses me goodbye and hoists his pack. "Know what I'll always remember about you?" It was his favorite part from our night on the plywood. At least this time he has the decency to whisper it in my ear.


OVER TEA AND TOAST with Aussie Ann the next day, I'm feeling kind of mopey. My stomach is also off, pitching and heaving like a storm's moving in.

"Are you going to Sumatra?" she asks.

"Still not sure." Sumatra is wild and primitive, hard traveling, the next step in my evolution as an Overlander. Am I ready for it?

Suddenly a sharp cramp doubles me over. Sweat beads up on my forehead, I'm shivering, then everything disappears for a moment.

When my vision clears, I'm peering into Aussie Ann's baby blues. "What's wrong, luv? You all right?"

Somebody's tugging my arm. A tiny, elderly Javanese woman has snuck onto the veranda and crept up to us, palm outstretched.

"I don't feel so good." I pitch forward and the tiny lady kneels, rubbing my belly and clucking sympathetically.

Eventually the spasm subsides. I pass the old woman my plate, tell her *makan*, take a deep breath and try to resume conversation with Ann.

When our guest has finished my toast, she picks up my camera and motions she'd like to take our picture.

I haul myself up and we pose against the porch railing, me looking like death warmed over, Ann like she's off to a Junior League picnic.

After breakfast I choke down some charcoal tablets—said to absorb and flush the impurities from the system—then collapse in Cliff's room with chills and fever, excruciating cramps and severe nausea.

Hours pass. I drag myself to the *mandi*, guzzle tin cupfuls of the boiled water set out for us to brush our teeth. Nothing stays down. Now I'm too weak and shaky to stand, crawling on all fours across the damp concrete floor to the drain.

Everything is black here, the sand, the rice, the puke.

More hours pass; fitful sleep interrupted by periods of wakefulness and torment. I drain several teapots of boiled water. Towards dusk, shivering in the heat, I ask the manager for more.

"*You* are drinking this all day? You are not well?" This earns me the VIP treatment. A metal wastebasket is delivered to the room. Trembling, I wrap myself in Cliff's blanket and watch the curtains drift, the daylight dim, miserably awaiting the moment I'll have to lean over and put it to use.

LATER. Light from the doorway, people at my bedside, a lamp being switched on. Coralee, back from a walkabout of the countryside. I'd kiss her feet if I trusted myself to move.

She takes in the deluxe room, the vases of flowers, me shivering on the double bed, metal wastebasket close at hand. She'd left me a week ago in a windowless cell with a 40-watt bare bulb.

"When I see travelers like this, I tell them they must go hospital," says the manager. "She cannot last through the night this way." He gestures ominously at the wastebasket.

She glances inside. "Why is it black?"

"Charcoal. I chewed charcoal tablets, I heard that's supposed to help."

"Charcoal can absorb certain poisons," Coralee says. "But fever and chills—bacterial infection—it's no use for that."

"Go hospital," the manager repeats. "Not Muslim one, that poor people. Go Dutch hospital, Christian. Bethesda. Take *becak*. Three hundred *rupes*."

I pull on a sundress and jean jacket, take my passport and some traveler's checks, then padlock everything else with Cliff's stuff.

Coralee raises her eyebrows at the men's clothes: Attagirl! But outside she's all business.

"BETHESDA HOSPITAL," she bellows at a bunch of drivers smoking beside their bicycle carriages. "*Seratus lima puluh!*" Howls, snickers, counteroffers: Coralee stands her ground.

Finally someone pedals over. I raise *my* eyebrows: attagirl. "Right on sister. A hundred and fifty!"

"You have to know how to talk to these people," she quotes Snotty Girl. "Three hundred my arse."

We clamber into the carriage and the driver pedals like crazy over potholed streets in the close, humid night while I clutch the railing and try not to hurl.

The hospital entrance is surrounded by earthquake rubble and orderlies smoking cigarettes, but whatever the driver shouts causes them to spring into action like wind-up dolls.

The men in white coats ungently transfer me to a vintage World War I stretcher and careen through the hallways in search of the hospital's lone doctor on call, wheels clattering, while I gaze up at the faraway fluorescent lights.

The ceiling is floating, but not in that nice mushroom-y way. I'm delirious, screaming at myself. "INDONESIA. Ya hadda fuckin' come to INDONESIA!"

In the exam room, the doctor questions me in the clipped, British intonation of one schooled in colonial times.

"Have you been inoculated against cholera?" I had, actually, not that I remembered this at the moment. He swabs off a rectal thermometer.

"You don't have an oral...cholera? Oh my God. I have CHOLERA?"

The doctor smiles. "Not likely, or you would be dead by now." He gestures to my midsection. "This is why I never travel abroad. Foreign flora and fauna create havoc in the system." He reads the thermometer. "Thirty-nine."

That's maybe not good. *"Panas?"*

*"Panas,"* he agrees. "Hot. You are dehydrated, you have a bacterial infection. With some medication, some saline, you'll soon be good as new."

I'm wheeled to a private room with a window onto the courtyard that looks like heaven at first but becomes my own private purgatory soon thereafter.

Throughout the night, I'm attended by an army of giggling incompetents, not trained healthcare workers so much as girls wearing white shirtwaists and oxfords.

None of them can insert the IV needle or find a vein. After puncturing my hands repeatedly, they give up and switch to a leg.

The entire night shift is now gathered in my room. Each dimwit takes a turn and fails as everyone else laughs.

"*DIMANA DOKTER!*" I scream. More laughter.

Finally, awakened by all the ruckus, a woman in a nurse's cap comes in, jabs my leg and starts the drip.

For the rest of the night, someone comes in every 20 minutes and switches on the overhead light. Every time I scream. This delights them; it becomes a game. I doze off, they take turns startling me awake. If I weren't dying myself, I'd have murdered them.

I awaken to the entire day shift clustered around my bed. "Hi, lady!" an orderly says. "You from Australia?"

"FUCK OFF." My leg is throbbing now, red, swollen, hot to the touch. Dirty needles. I'm going to get hepatitis. "GET THE DOCTOR!" I point to my leg. The group scatters, chortling with glee.

Another woman in a white hat comes in and grates my leg with rubbing alcohol. It stings horribly.

"STOP THAT! *DOKTER! DIMANA DOKTER!*" As I'm screaming it occurs to me that I couldn't have carried on like this yesterday. I must be feeling better.

The doctor, when he finally arrives, agrees. "You're coming along nicely. We can take you off the IV. Your temperature is normal."

I show him my leg. "See what your 'nurses' did to me?" Air quotes.

He lays a soothing hand on my inflamed calf, not acknowledging the maltreatment or the air quotes.

"I'll order a salve for this. And we can start you on a bland diet." He's leaving now. "You'll soon be good as new."

"When can I get out of here?" I call after him.

A tray arrives, a plated mound of what looks like, but probably is not mashed potatoes, with greasy liquid congealed in a little pool at the top. Up and over this heap of slop a line of ants are traveling.

"TAKE IT AWAY!" I scream, making shooing motions.

The teenager who brought it in backs out of the room, mystified that I've turned down my meal.

Coralee visits in the afternoon. I show her my infected leg and tell her I'd been served insects for lunch.

"And to think this is considered the upmarket hospital in town!" She's marveling at the equipment now, like she's at a museum. "Though you actually do seem better."

By the next morning it's clear that the novelty of caring for the foreigner has worn off. I'm no longer funny or interesting, just difficult. The dynamic has shifted: whereas before I had too much attention, now I can't get any.

Okay, I'll just start walking out. Like when a restaurant keeps you waiting for your check too long. Always works. There's just one problem. I can't find my clothes. They have taken my clothing, confiscated my very humanity: "MY CLOTHES!" I scream. "*Dimana pakaian?*"

The young woman who responds to this latest disturbance actually appears to grasp the situation: no clothes.

"*Nanti*," she says.

So my clothes are at the *nanti?* Where is that? "*Dimana nanti!*" I demand.

She looks puzzled by the question.

"WHERE ARE MY CLOTHES!" I'm ranting again; trapped, helpless. I must escape this "hospital" with its ants in the food, these imbeciles in white dresses wielding dirty needles. THE COURTYARD! I race through the corridor in my hospital gown, screaming *Dimana nanti!* with the nurse-imposter on my heels.

Outside, visiting families and recovering patients are milling about. Lush plantings, shaded benches, the perfect place to stage a loud, public scene.

"*Nanti!*" The girl calls. "*NANTI!*"

I whirl around and say *where-the-hell-is-my-stuff* through clenched teeth.

"No Ingrish," she says.

So I start mocking her, mean-spiritedly I admit, since she's just trying to help: "*Habla Espanol? Parlez vous Francais? Sprechen sie Deutsch?*"

The girl brightens. "Dutch," she says. "Dutch! *Nanti!*"

She returns with a little grey-haired lady in a flowered-print duster like my gramma wears—a patient, not the person of authority I was expecting.

"Dutch!" *Nanti*-girl keeps repeating, like this woman is the answer to my problems.

"*Sprechen Sie Deutsch?*" I ask.

She understands me. "*Niet Duits. Nederlands.*"

I understand her. Not German, Dutch.

Speaking slowly and pantomiming broadly, we discover we can communicate. My new friend tells me she's 'about' 70. She learned Dutch as a little girl in school. She has cancer. "*Krebs.*" She gestures to her breasts.

I show her my leg and tell her about the ant-infested meal.

I let them bring me food? She shudders. "*Mijn familie brengt eten.*"

When I ask where my clothes are, and where this *nanti* is, the girl bursts in with a torrent of Bahasa and much gesticulating.

"*Ze wassen uw kleding.*" The old woman pantomimes scrubbing at a wash-board, hanging clothes on a line. "*Niet droog.*" Not dry. "*Wachten.*" Wait. "'*Nanti*' bedacht '*wachten.*'"

So. 'Nanti' means 'wait,' my clothes are being washed, and I'm an asshole. That being said, I still have no clothes.

Through my interpreter, I plead with the girl to bring my dress, RIGHT NOW. It can dry while I'm wearing it.

Clothed in my damp dress, I'm shown to a room where an Important Person at a Big Desk is stamping paperwork in many places: my hospital bill.

They charged me for the uneaten insects, but I don't even object. Two nights in a private room, meds and doctor visits come to under 30 bucks. I take out my Traveller's Checques and lay down two fresh twenties.

Important Guy sighs. "No trapel check." I show him that I have only a couple crumpled 100 *rupe* notes. He nods. Very well. I have demonstrated the means and the intent to pay; accommodations will be made. I am escorted outside.

A white VW bus with a red cross painted on the side—the hospital's sole ambulance—will transport me to the bank downtown.

Onboard I find *nanti* girl canoodling with the ambulance driver. There's a hospital orderly in back. It's a joyride!

We careen through the streets, dodging potholes and scattering the pushcarts, whizzing through the traffic roundabouts with lights flashing. I'm whisked to the front of the currency exchange queue, turning the heads of two Brits in a classic double-take as we race past.

"TRISH!" I yell. "TREVOR! Remember me?" It's the teachers I'd met my first day in Bali.

"The girl from Chicago," I hear Trish say. "With the traveler's checks?"

"Ah yes. Hallo, Yankee bird. Ask for small denominations. ACCEPT NO BILL OVER 1000!" Trevor shouts.


Coralee and I spend her last night in Jogja ensconced in Cliff's room, taking artfully-posed photos of each other reflected in the mirror, with masses of fallen flower petals framing each shot.

The next morning she's dressed like when I first met her, in a flowered skirt and jean jacket. The holidays are coming. She has to be getting home.

We perform the final Overland ritual: exchange our full names, addresses and home phones, knowing there is no likelihood we'll ever get in touch.

It's our way of telling someone our time together had meant something; that we'd made a connection, that we wanted to remember each other.

Cool-headed and competent, always one to downplay the drama of the moment in favor of a practical solution, Coralee has been an ideal travel partner.

We say goodbye in the language we'd struggled with together. She tells me stay well: "*Selamat tingaal.*"

Go well, I answer. "*Selamat jalan.*"


THE WEEKEND BEFORE CHRISTMAS, the Overlanders are crammed back-to-back at Helen's café and some guy keeps banging his chair into mine—a fine-looking guy, I can't help but notice, blond and freshly permed.

"Could you please move?"

He's with three other guys, Germans all. They've been drinking heavily.

"YOU'RE AMERICAN, RIGHT?" He spreads his arms wide. "AMERICA! Mickey Mouse! Wonder Bread!"

I roll my eyes, which seems to egg him on.

"BASEBALL! APPLE PIE!" His arms knock into my chair.

"Shut up, Frank," says one of the men.

"COCA-COLA! ROCK-AND-ROLL!" Frank dissolves into a fit of giggles while I remain trapped.

"Wow," I say. "You're really drunk."

He cracks up. He has an adorable smile. "And really cute," I hear myself saying. The buddies all smirk: here we go again.

He asks my name and where I'm staying. "Want to go on a date, American girl? A disco date? I pick you up tomorrow, 7 o'clock."

"A date? Oh for sure. That'll happen." In my experience, boys this drunk and this cute never call the next day.

Which is why I'm surprised to find him in the lounge at the Kota the next morning, fresh as a daisy and sober as a judge. He stubs his cigarette and stands as I approach.

"Good morning! Today we go Christmas shopping."

We wander the stalls on the *jalan* as Frank explain he now lives in Sweden, where the lifestyle is more to his liking. "I have told my Fatherland *auf wiedersehen*! You do not buy any gifts?"

I look into his blue Aryan eyes and explain just why, in his mother tongue, I do not celebrate Christmas. "*Ich bin Jüdisch. Ich Weihnachten nicht feiern.*"

He cocks an eyebrow.

"Surprised?"

"Yes! Your pronunciation is excellent!"

And so it will be with every German I meet. The Holocaust is off the table. I will not assign, nor would they accept, any blame for the sins of their fathers.


Frank returns for our date dressed like the boys back home out for a Saturday night: in tight white flairs, platform clogs and a collared, short-sleeved shirt with several buttons undone. Clean-shaven and doused in Paco Rabanne, he's a standout among the grungy slobs that populate the Trail.

I've taken some extra effort with my appearance as well. I'm wearing makeup and have applied some closely hoarded creme rinse post-shampoo.

"You look beautiful," Frank says. "Very romantical."

He insists we find someone to take our picture and strikes a pose—shoulders back, chin down, one leg extended and hand on hip, a man who's clearly spent some time in front of the camera—then beckons me to step inside the frame.

Our disco date is a blast. We do the Bump, the Hustle, the Latin Hustle. We lead a Soul Train line dance. And all the while his posse looks on from the sidelines, smoking and drinking, speaking only amongst themselves.

Later, we're sitting on his bottom bunk paging through an album of blurry Instamatic shots chronicling all the places he's been, or more accurately, all the girls he's met.

"Mykonos." Canadian redhead. "Penang." Norwegian blonde. When this roll is developed I suppose another girl will be looking over his shoulder and he'll be pointing at me: "Jogjakarta."

He shows me a gorgeous Thai girl—'Phuket'— and watches my reaction. "Do you notice anything special about this girl? Look closely." He taps the picture. "This girl, she is no lady."

I'd gathered that. "You mean, she's a hooker?"

"I mean, she's a HE!" he shrieks.

"Gimme that!" I grab the album. Phuket Girl has long black hair, beautiful complexion and delicate features. Anyone would have fallen for her.

"Imagine when I finally find out. BIG surprise."

We're having lots of laughs but as the night proceeds Frank gets kind of twitchy.

I pass him a joint. He hesitates, takes a quick puff and refuses more. Our eyes meet. He leans in, pecks me on the cheek, then jumps up and excuses himself.

He returns after quite a while, highly agitato. "I see you back to your hotel now."

So. I'm beautiful, I'm romantical, and I'm going home now.

This is strange. But of no consequence. I'm leaving tomorrow, on the night train to Jakarta.

"All righty then." I take his politely extended hand.

My date offers me his arm and escorts me back to the Kota, carefully guiding us around puddles that would muddy his white slacks.

This is more strange. The next day he's back. No mention of the night before.

We run errands, have lunch, browse the street stalls hand in hand, then he sees me to the train.

Amid the tumult—the train whistling, steam billowing, the *becak* drivers hustling fares—Frank writes his contact information on a page of notebook paper.

He folds it carefully, asks for mine, tucks my address in his shirt pocket. The train starts chugging, loud, fast, louder, faster, till an ear-splitting whistle mobilizes the throngs.

As everyone starts pushing onto the cars, Frank steps forward, takes both my hands in his, and bows.

# jakarta

December 22, 1975

Chaos.

No one ever has a good word to say about Jakarta.

The heat is oppressive, the pollution toxic; it's impossible to navigate.

One visits the capital only on urgent business—which I have—and passes through with all deliberate speed—which I will. Because standing beside me, waiting to detrain, stands Holman.

My white knight is Batak, tall and good-looking, with impeccable English. I'd met and immediately clicked with various Batak kids enrolled at the university in Jogja. Natives of Sumatra, they were brilliant students, every one of them an artist, a dancer, or musician; we'd played some music together.

I hoist my guitar onto my shoulder. "I went to Batak recitals in Jogja. Learned to play some songs."

He nods. "Music and dance—our culture—is very important to us—" and looks me over, loaded down with baggage, yellow guidebook in hand, suffering in the heat. "Do you need help getting somewhere?

I tell him I'm catching the six o'clock ferry. "Twelve hours. Plenty of time."

"Twelve hours? You'll never make it."

Carrying my luggage overhead he leads me through the crowds to the ferry office in Jakarta's historic center, waits with me in line, gets me booked General Passage on the two-night voyage and escorts me to the business district, where, among turn-of-the-century colonial buildings and single-story homes and shops, with Javanese peaked roofs, a few gleaming skyscrapers now loom.

He waits patiently as I check at both the post office and American Express for mail being held in my name. None is found. Oh well. At least the office was air-conditioned.

"You seem very disappointed," Holman says. He's a law student, fascinated by and well-versed in American history and politics. "So you're from Chicago?" This question is almost always followed by pretend tommy-gun fire. But instead he says, "Your city hosted an exciting political convention a few years back."

"Oh, it was exciting all right. I was there for a while. Till the police started swinging their sticks." Then I'd gone home to watch the rest of the convention in the rec room, on TV. I was only 17, just getting into the whole demonstration scene.

"That convention led to a lengthy court battle," Holman says.

"The Chicago 7 trial? A TRAVESTY. Presided by Judge Julius Hoffman, an idiot who never heard of the Constitution."

He shifts my valise to his left shoulder. "And what about the other Hoffman?"

"Abbie?" His antics had embarrassed me. I wanted our movement to be taken seriously. He'd made it into a charade.

"I actually met him that day. He was standing next to a drinking fountain in Lincoln Park, reading some anarchist manifesto off a sheet of notebook paper. Also an idiot."

"That was my impression." Holman sighs. "A country so blessed with freedom—to make such mockery of it…"

When my business is concluded Holman invites me to his home for a traditional Batak meal. "My family awaits my arrival. We would be honored for you to join us."

We walk through a neighborhood where sewage flows alongside unpaved streets and chickens roam free—a shortcut, I assume, to the upscale area where he lives— but a moment later he stops in front of a tiny wooden box with a tile roof and iron grilles spanning a couple narrow openings in the wall.

"This"—with a sweep of his hand—"is my home."

I shift my face into neutral, like when someone shows you a picture of their ugly baby. He's serious. He's proud of this house, and finally, after hearing all my life that we have the world's highest standard of living, I get it.

Here's two people standing in the same place. One of them sees a middle-class residential area; the other, a slum.

MOM AND GRANDMA SEEM NONE TOO PLEASED That their boy has returned from university with a bare-armed, blue-jean-wearing Yankee girl in tow.

They scowl and won't look at me directly, but Holman is the man of the house and his word is law.

They exchange formal greetings, then Holman issues instructions that send Grandma to a cupboard for another place setting.

"Lunch will be served shortly. In the meantime," he looks me up and down pointedly, "you may use the W.C to freshen up."

A night in third-class on a Third World train and a morning of tramping around the muddy streets of Jakarta in blistering heat have done nothing to enhance my appearance. A shower would be great.

With a grim expression of unmasked resentment, Mom hands me a thin towel and points me to the *mandi*—a barrel of water, with a washtub draining through the floor to the ditch outside, and a squat toilet, and me still expecting a shower. Why? Because I *still* don't get it.

I clean up as best possible and emerge in a long-sleeved tunic, my hair pony-tailed, wearing lip gloss and blush.

Holman's face brightens. "Now you look very charming." He rises to seat me at a table laden with many small bowls of unappetizing, unidentifiable foodstuff: Padang food. I should have made this connection. The Batak are from Sumatra.

Later I'll learn other Batak recipes include dog and horse meat simmered in the animal's blood; also that the Batak were still practicing ritual cannibalism when the Portuguese arrived: if this is, they have certainly evolved.

Now that I'm cleaned up Holman broaches another topic. "Why do you Western travelers go around looking so unkempt?" He passes the rice. "Why can you not present a nicer appearance, as guests in another country?"

I stammer something about the places we stay lacking adequate facilities to bathe and do laundry, then attempt to backpedal. The facilities are identical to the ones I just used.

The reality I cannot admit—that we're accustomed to long hot showers in tiled bathrooms, washing machines and dryers, worst case scenario, a Laundromat—that kneeling over a galvanized steel washtub you fill up at an outdoor spigot, then drag to a patch of dry ground while it sloshes all over you is more effort than most Overlanders—predominantly guys—are willing to expend.

"Why would you stay in such places, then?" he presses. "Surely you have the means to stay in lodgings with every modern convenience."

"Yes, but we're trying to extend our travels as long as possible, so we try to spend as little..."

His eyes narrow. How spoiled and indulgent this must sound to a striving, ambitious young man with no time off to spare.

I make show of appearing to sample from every bowl on the table, fill up on rice and tea and thank Holman's mother and grandmother.

"*Terima kasih.*" I bob my head respectfully and bid them stay well. "*Selamat tinggaal.*"

They look relieved and wish me safe travel. "*Selamat jalan.*"


Holman leads me alongside the sewage ditches to the main thoroughfare, where we board a bus for the main port in North Jakarta.

There the massive *Tamponas* stands moored at the dock on the stinking waters of Tanjung Priok harbor, with masses of humanity stampeding towards her. Ear- splitting blasts emanate from the monstrous ship. There are no orderly queues, nothing's roped off; pandemonium.

The people who booked general passage are pushing onto the first-class gangplank, the first-class passengers are pushing back, and it's high time I joined the fray.

When I turn to thank Holman he asks for my picture. I offer him one from Bali showing me in a sarong, my face in profile.

"Not this one! You can't even tell you're white!"

I'm trying to conserve my extra passport photos for visa applications, but that's the one he wants, a head shot showing me in my own native attire—a turtleneck sweater and jean jacket.

I should have asked to take his picture but my Olympus Pen is buried in my bag and I'm eager to board, so I will have nothing to remember him by except his kindness.

THE FERRY IS SEVERAL STORIES HIGH, with about a 2,500-passenger capacity and 3,000 aboard. Families with their cargo: food and newspaper-wrapped parcels tied in colorful plastic twine. I show my ticket and passport at the bottom of the gangplank and inch along at a 45-degree angle, excitement mounting. I've never been on an actual ship. It seems such an old-fashioned, romantic way to travel, like something out of an old newsreel.

The uniformed man at the top of the ramp glances at my passport and stamps my ticket. I ask him where to go: *dimana saya pergi?*

He turns to the next passenger.

A couple of backpackers point me towards a non-working escalator.

"They said the Americans are supposed to go upstairs to the first-class deck."

"First class? Right on!" Does it occur to me to question why we're entitled to such privilege when the Indonesians traveling general passage are being sent to steerage, in the bowels of the ship? Not for a moment. The path to enlightenment is not a straight line.

On the first-class deck we catch a delicious ocean breeze and magnificent view of the city. North lies the Java Sea. I make camp on the gleaming teak floorboards, spreading my second-hand blue batik as a sheet while wearing my day pack containing my passport, traveler's checks, notebooks, camera and books.

I leave in my humongous trunk my radio, clock and cheap Woolworth's wallet, which contains the last of my Indonesian cash—about 2,000 *rupes* in folding money and another 300 or so in change, my Illinois driver's license and Student Travel ID.

Hours pass; the deck fills up. Aussies, Germans, Dutch, Brits; an Italian contingent, we three Yanks and two Indonesian boys who've snuck past the crew.

I read, try to tune in the BBC, strum the guitar. I light a clove cigarette from the full pack I'd splurged on, then wander over to the rail briefly to look down at the water. Six o'clock comes and goes, the sun sets. No movement. By now I'm crazy thirsty and hungry, and the mess hall is open, so I walk back a few feet to my suitcase to get some cash.

I can't find my wallet.

Did I not put it in this compartment? Did I move it to the day pack? I go through everything, heart racing, sweat beading along my hairline. Nothing looks disturbed. When could anyone have gotten their hands on my stuff? I've been right near it the whole time. My stomach is looping now, my temples throbbing and feet tingling: full panic mode. I can't find my damn wallet.

My new pack of Djarums are gone also. I haven't misplaced anything, I've been robbed.

Immediately I started talking myself down. About $5.50 in cash has been stolen. My traveler's checks, passport, everything important is safe.

Deep breath. *Fear is the mind killer.* OK, so I'll change another Traveller's Cheque on the ship. I'm out five bucks. What really bothers me is that the thief is nearby, watching me that very moment, no doubt. A fellow traveler? One of our brotherhood?

Unthinkable.

Scanning the vicinity, I reluctantly conclude the only ones close enough to have gone through my stuff for the couple moments my back was turned are the two Indonesian boys.

I saunter up to them. "Hi. How's it goin'?" Kids who hang around Westerners usually speak English.

"Good evening," they say, all polite.

"Did you guys notice anyone going through my gear? My wallet is missing."

They look back and forth, all wide-eyed. "No."

"Aw gee." Big sigh, fake. "Thing is, I need that wallet. If you see anybody with it, maybe you could tell them they should keep the money, but the Yank chick really needs her wallet back. Okay?"

Okay, they'll do that for me.

Down many flights of stationary escalators is the cafeteria, where a guy is plopping small, unappetizing mounds of a food-like substance on paper plates.

I show him a $10 Traveller's Cheque.

"No Trapel Check," he snarls. "Rupiah." I ask where I can change money.

"No Ingrish." He motions for me to scram.

A woman draped in several sarongs, one of which contains a baby, taps me on the shoulder and points out a man in a white short-sleeved shirt, navy blue pants and cap with an insignia. "Ingrish."

I approach the official with my Traveller's Checque and ask where I can change money.

"The bursar's office. But it is closed now. And they do not take Trapel Check, only cash."

I can forego eating for a couple days, particularly that slop I've just seen, but I can't go without liquid for 48 hours. This voyage isn't going so well, and we haven't even left port yet.

Loud bursts of static cut through the general din: there's a PA system.

"Can you make an announcement over the loudspeaker?" He nods. What would I like him to say? He will make an announcement, but right now he must check on the passengers below deck. Would I accompany him?

We descend to steerage.

Hundreds of people have spread blankets and batiks over the patches of wet concrete they'll be sleeping on for the next two nights. Baskets and parcels define each family's turf. Fluorescent tubes provide harsh overhead light. There's no ventilation. The air is stale. Passengers and packages and food, in a basement flowing with bilge; the odor hangs there with nowhere else to go.

Yet the people look happy, satisfied with their surroundings and the general progress of the voyage. They're taking out their dinners, packaged in old newspaper, shouting and laughing, running after their babies.

I'm trying to imagine what will induce everyone to quiet down, snuggle up on the damp concrete and nod off later tonight.

Amidst the hubbub, my captain translates my plea for the wallet's safe return, scribbling on the margins of an official sheet attached to a clipboard. Patiently he crosses out a phrase or two as I edit, never saying what a ridiculous idea this is, assuring me the carefully crafted announcement will be made: if it is, I will have no clue.


When I return to my little campsite, I smooth out my blue batik and push my valise against the bulwark.

There beneath it, with the folding money removed, but still containing my Illinois driver's license, Student Travel ID and 300 rupiah in change, is my wallet.

# chicago

December 30, 2015

## Starting at the Finish Line

I got on that flight in 1975 an American and got off a Yank.

Yank-baiting was a popular pastime in the months after we'd fled Saigon with Ho on our heels. Americans abroad faced constant disapproval, scorn and derision. From finger-pointing range. We were challenged daily to justify US policies we abhorred, to defend our shamed president and unjust war; even fellow Overlanders cut us no slack.

"You're absolutely right." I pointed back. "That war was a national disgrace." Their faces would fall: I wouldn't take the bait. "Nixon? Don't get me started."

Agreeing with the antagonists never failed to disarm them. Spoiled all their fun.

In those days of raging anti-American sentiment you'd think we'd have been ostracized on the Trail. But it was quite the opposite. We were the center of attention, the life of every party, the coolest of the cool—or so we believed—

if only because, myself excluded, our passports had the most stamps. We had come the furthest; we'd been gone the longest, and these were two of the top three measures of status along the Hippie Trail.

The third was how small a daily budget you were able to maintain, on average. This category the Germans totally dominated, no contest.

I stumbled onto the scene hardly a month off US soil, cashless and clueless, to be met by veteran travelers not with disdain, but open arms. I brought news from home. Who won the World Series? Who's this Gerald Ford? Has the baby been born on *All in the Family*?

I brought entertainment: a guitar, playing cards, books to trade. I'd even unwittingly packed the only available real- time link with the outside world. Once word got out a Yank chick had a transistor radio that could frequently tune in the BBC, I was never at a loss for company at 6 o'clock.

Even for those pre-internet days, our isolation was profound. No TV, practically zero English-language print—a two-week-old edition of the International Herald Tribune would go on a waiting list—of course, no phones—and by phones, I mean *land lines.*

This is the part of the story Millennials can't fathom. You didn't make reservations? You couldn't just *call home*?

That was travel in an Informationless Age. In places the phone lines didn't reach and the guidebooks didn't cover, our #1 source of intel was the people coming from the other direction. In distant second place was the ill-researched, scarcely available *Southeast Asia on a Shoestring*, The Book we loved to hate that would evolve into a highly reliable multi-channel travel guide empire called Lonely Planet.

Apart from the rare telegram the only way to communicate with home was through the mail.

Parents sent mail addressed *Poste Restante, Hold for Arrival*, to postal facilities or American Express offices, then wondered whether the letter—or the kid—ever arrived.

We wrote home on the tissue-paper mailers my parents saved for all those years. I would think of them waiting for those letters when decades later, my husband texted me a notification from the bank. Funds had been withdrawn from an airport ATM in Manchester; I could rest assured our son just landed safely in England for his junior year abroad.

Reading my journal entries and those old letters, I'm amazed by how kindly I was treated. Total strangers, locals and other Overlanders, took me in and guided me along, and asked so little in return: a photo, a conversation, a song. I'm also stunned by how trusting I was, never questioning anyone's intentions or fearing for my safety. My biggest concern seems to have been finding a bathroom—or dependable directions, a clean drink of water. A place to sleep.

Today we have bottled water, the Internet, smart phones on par with any tricorder from the starship Enterprise. We have information; we are empowered. We travel, and live, knowing up front what risks are involved.

Then, we knew squat. We assumed we were safe, yet buses broke down and planes crashed and boats sank and nobody took responsibility for anyone's safety.

This first came to my attention in 1981, six years after I'd ferried out of Jakarta. The Tamponas II sank in the Java Sea. U.S papers all ran the story. A fire started in the cargo hold and sparked an explosion; there were 1,054 registered passengers and no lifeboats aboard, because the Pelni line routinely stripped their ships of "unnecessary equipment" to carry as many passengers as possible.

Passing vessels rescued 649 passengers and crew who'd been able to jump from the upper decks, but because hundreds of passengers crammed in the hold weren't included in the official count, the true tally of how many perished will never be known.

I wasn't sure which aspect of this account bothered me more—the fact that I could have gone down on that ship, or that I might have been outside on the first-class deck with the white people when that fire started, and I could have jumped.

Years later on the internet I'll find images of the ship that don't jive with the stately vessel of my recollection, and I'll discover I had crossed on the older big sister, the Tamponas I, that didn't sink. That had carried even more passengers in cargo, with no lifeboats.

Progress has eradicated most of the unique culture and old-fashioned charm of these destinations. But what remains is being preserved, and that is also progress. Decrepit shrines and historic buildings, restored to their original glory; natural resources are being protected. Taman Sari, where Cliff and I clambered over dilapidated walls choked with weeds, has been reclaimed and designated a World Heritage site. Mount Bromo, where Coralee and I trudged through the mist is now a national park. Similar initiatives are being undertaken in natural areas and historic districts described in chapters to follow.

Sadly, the decades have not been kind to Indonesia. Her islands have withstood earthquakes and volcanic eruptions, been engulfed by tsunamis causing loss of life beyond comprehension, and—most tragic of all, because this is man's doing—Jakarta is sinking.

Some streets of North Jakarta where Holman and I walked forty years ago are submerged 13½ feet beneath the sea. To save their city, Indonesia plans to build a Great Sea Wall. It's a planned joint venture with the people best-qualified to help, who owe a debt from the past, who began reclaiming their nation from the sea a thousand years ago, one spoonful at a time, so the legend goes: Indonesia's former colonizers, the dike-building Dutch.

Today, safe in my inland home, shielded by faraway mountain ranges, upon no major fault lines along the shoreline of the world's largest freshwater system, I wonder when we will act to save the other sinking coastal cities around the world, and whether Holman's tiny home has withstood the deluge.

# singapore

## December 24, 1975

**C**ivilization.

On the shuttle into Singapore Harbor, a Yank I didn't meet onboard engrossed in a John Fowles I haven't read notices me studying the cover of his paperback.

"*The French Lieutenant's Woman.* Have you read it?"

"Not that one, but all his others."

"You can have it when I'm finished."

When he's closed the book and folded his reading glasses into a shirt pocket he introduces himself: Paul, from Alexandria, Virginia; FBI, retired.

"FBI. Uh-huh."

He laughs and passes me his gold badge. Hefty, in a leather case, it looks authentic and so does Paul. Fit and trim, with craggy features, a neat mustache and a few silver strands in his dark blond hair, he's quite a convincing G-man.

We'd had dramatically different shipboard experiences. Paul had slept in a bed. He seems upset by my robbery and the starvation rations I've been on the past couple days, and disturbed by my description of the airless, foul- smelling cargo hold with hordes of people packed together on wet concrete.

"They had hundreds of passengers over capacity jammed in steerage?" He shakes his head. "Unbelievable. Here." He passes me the book. "You'll really enjoy this."

Standing beside FBI Paul makes clearing customs a breeze. He presents his passport and flips open the badge, receives a respectful nod and is waved through.

A glance over his shoulder at me gets my passport stamped and bag chalked with nary a peek. So I never experience the intrusive search and questioning that puts so many Overlanders off Singapore. In other lines, guys with hair longer than collar-length are emptying pockets and presenting onward tickets, backpackers' money is being counted and gear unpacked; all these indignities I'm spared because I'm standing alongside a respectable-looking man.

"You have a reservation? I'm at the Strand, you could stay there."

"Not on *my* budget."

"Hey, it's Christmas Eve. It's on me."

Split-second decision time. Paul seems nice, FBI and all. He has great taste in reading material. He could be a pervert, or a serial killer, or just what he appears—a pleasant middle-aged man who doesn't want to spend Christmas alone. My gut says go.

We taxi down the pristine harbor front to the Strand. The traffic is sedate, controlled by stoplights. Street signs in Bahasa Malay, English, Chinese and Hindi leave no room for ambiguity. Pedestrians stroll the wide walkways, accustomed to behaving themselves.

Paul suggests dinner in Chinatown, a fantastic idea, I tell him, as Jewish dietary law dictates the Christmas Eve consumption of Chinese food.

"You're a nut. Y'know that?" He opens the door. "After you."

Chinatown is a couple blocks and a century removed from the sparkling, modern harbor: noisy, dirty, chaotic, authentic. Barbecued ducks swing by their necks in the sidewalk shanties fronting dilapidated Victorian buildings the Brits left behind. Brightly colored silks and trinkets are sold in stalls lining narrow streets bustling with enterprise. We're seated at a table on the street as the sun goes down.

Paul puts on his reading glasses and scans the menu. "Bottle of wine? What do you like, white?"

"GREAT! I haven't had wine in months."

"You been on the wagon?"

"Nope, just the Hippie Trail."

He smiles and looks over the top of his glasses at the waiter. "What's good tonight?"

"Chilli crab," the man barks. "Lobstah noodoo. Crispy duck pancake." A slight nod from Paul sends him rushing to the kitchen.

When the dishes arrive, wafting steam redolent of garlic and pepper, anise and nutmeg I practically swoon. I raise the bowl to my face Asian-style and start shoveling fried rice like I'm going to the Chair.

"You sure can wield a pair of chopsticks, little lady."

Night falls. The proprietor lights our candle and switches on the colored bulbs strung alongside the tables.

Darkness becomes Chinatown. It conceals all the garbage and grime, the passage of time. And I must say it has a similar effect on Paul. With his lines and creases obscured, he's quite a handsome man.

He's also generous, chivalrous, an attentive listener, and completely unforthcoming about his personal life. All I can get from him is that he's divorced and it wasn't amicable.

"There's some used-book stalls around here." Paul signals for the check, topic closed. "Want to take a look?"

We plunder tables heaped with everything from near-current pulp fiction to gilt-edged hardbound classics, a paperback leaps out at me: *The Great Railway Bazaar: By Train Through Asia,* by Paul Theroux—the future star of train travel writing.

We dive into our books and separate beds at the Strand, reading in companionable silence, until the eyelids start to droop. He switches off the bedside lamp and I wind my little clock.

"Paul?" I whisper in the dark. "It's close to midnight. Merry Christmas."

"Merry Christmas," he whispers back.

"Thanks for making this such a special night. I'll never forget it."

"Me either, doll."

ON CHRISTMAS MORNING I move into the Shang Onn, a crumbling mansion-turned-fleabag right down the street from historic Raffles hotel, in the heart of Singapore's colonial district. At a rate of about $4.00 US, it's safe—enough—and clean—enough. No bedbugs, just roaches and mice. With a single bed, low-watt lamp on a rickety nightstand and shared Western bath down the hallway, it suits me and my budget just fine.

Paul insists on shlepping my bag up a wide marble staircase that was probably once quite grand, his eyes darting back and forth in all the dark corners.

"You sure about this?"

"Yeah, why not?"

He looks at me for a long moment until he realizes I'm not kidding.

I wander Queen Elizabeth Walk the rest of Christmas Day, my foreign features attracting no attention. Anonymous and alone on the sidewalk, literally on the outside looking in, I think of Sunday morning bike rides back home, how I'd stop at the open windows of the neighborhood churches and listen. All those voices lifted in unison, singing in C major, so positive and forthright. So American. These are sounds of home, and I miss it today.

RAFFLES HOTEL, of world renown, has gotten run down.

Visitors, when there are any, enter through white marble colonnades and cross legendary Palm Court, stepping through a wrought-iron portico into a lobby resplendent in period furnishings.

Today, but for a couple other incurable romantics the place is empty.

The bartender, wiping down the gleaming teak of the famous Long Bar, knows exactly why I've come.

"Over there." He points out two vintage high-back rattan chairs. "Under those plaques. What's your drink?"

"Whatever's on tap."

He treats me to a tall, cold glass of water and draws me a mug of Tiger that I will nurse for hours at the table where Rudyard Kipling and W. Somerset Maugham once sat, drinking Singapore Slings.

Afterwards, I read discarded copies of the Straits Times from cover to cover and write letters by the deserted pool. The next day I return.

By Sunday night, I've posted all my letters and shipped a carton home. I've had film developed and clothes hand-laundered and seen Singapore's sights. Civilization! I've had enough of it.

Heading upstairs to my room above the restaurant, I cross Paul on the way down. He'd come to check on me.

"How are you getting along?"

"Great. Leaving tomorrow. How about a drink at the Long Bar?"

He's momentarily distracted by something scurrying in a corner. "Raffles?" He chuckles. "Lead the way."

The bartender has my tall, cold glass of water waiting by the time we reach the bar. He's been extremely tolerant of my lingering here for the last few days, parking in Mr. Maugham's chair, writing in a notebook and leaving minuscule tips, for he, too, is an Incurable Romantic, and we all kind of watch out for each other.

The water's purified," I tell Paul. "Even the ice."

The bartender folds his linen towel over his arm. "Would you like your pint of Tiger here, or at your table?"

Paul's head swivels, a classic straight-man take. "*Your* table?"

"Over there. See those plaques? Which chair would you like?"

He bobs his head back and forth, bringing the lettering into focus. "Definitely Rudyard Kipling."

"I figured."

The rattan chairs creak and rock that way they do as we settle into them. Paul sips his Singapore Sling. "You been staying in that rat trap and hanging around over here every day?"

I nod, I shrug.

"You're something else. You know that? So. What's next?"

"Tomorrow I'm catching the night train to Malaysia."

"You don't see much scenery from a night train," he says.

"But that way you save on a room."

"Oh. Of course. You gonna spring for a berth?"

"They have sleeping cars? YES!" I raise a soul fist. I am totally gonna dig Malaysia.

"Well then," he says. "Here's to you. Chin chin." And Paul raises his glass.

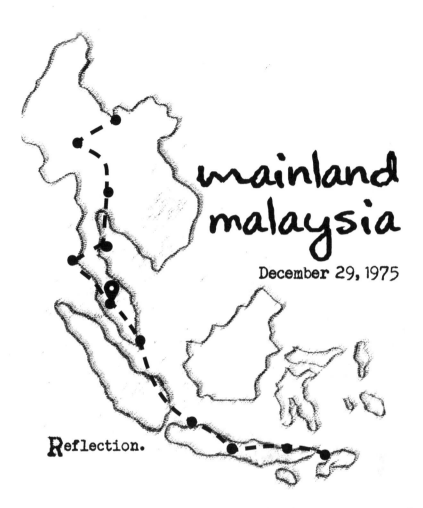

mainland
malaysia

December 29, 1975

**Reflection.**

Crossing Malaysia by rail is like being transported back to the days of the British Empire, to come to life in one of those black-and-white jungle movies starring Basil Rathbone in a pith helmet.

Singapore's Tanjong Pagar station is a time capsule that was sealed in 1932, an Art Deco monument, with foot- thick plaster walls to hold the heat at bay and Casablanca fans suspended from 72-foot ceilings. Expansive murals painted on rubber tiles depict scenes of colonial Malaya—workers planting rice, tapping rubber trees, mining tin. I'm in train buff, geography nerd heaven.

At the moment I'm also in Malaysia, which was awarded the station and the railway but not the land they stand on in an awkward divorce settlement 10 years earlier.

A bored-looking Malay customs official stamps me in— 14-day visitors' permit, no questions asked—then waves me towards the main hall where there's one brass ticket cage open, manned by a sullen Sikh.

"No sleepers available." Both his speech and manner are clipped. "Second-class through ticket to Bangkok"— he turns some pages—"$34.50 Malay." The exchange rate is an easy-to-calculate 40 cents per US dollar.

"So the sleepers are sold out?"

"No sleepers available," he repeats, both of us aware he hasn't answered the question. I must detrain in Kuala Lumpur; *yes*, there is a night train out of KL; *no*, he cannot sell me a berth, *yes*, travel checks are accepted, *for a fee*. Lots of scowling and stamping. A voluminous ticket folder and the equivalent of $13.80 US exchange hands.

The train is practically empty, an old narrow-gauge behind a locomotive that looks like it was converted from steam. There are no intimidating throngs elbowing their way onboard like on Tokyo's subways, no crush of shouting passengers packed shoulder-to-shoulder like on Hong Kong's buses and ferries, none of the chickens, bundles and babies cramming the floors, aisles and stairs of every Balinese and Javanese mode of transport.

We traverse a series of cast-iron overpasses above the roadways of downtown Singapore at a leisurely pace, then click past decommissioned colonial country stations in high disrepair, through palm-oil plantations that have surrendered to jungle, finally inching towards the kilometer-wide Causeway that links Singapore with peninsular Malaysia.

I squint at the tiny Atlas; confirmed. Across this bridge lies the southeastern tip of the Eurasian continent.

Proceeding through the verdant villages of Malaysia, each hamlet with its own small red-brick, tiled-roof country station set among the swaying palms and banana trees, I buy something at each stop. Here a deftly sliced chunk of fresh pineapple, there an F&N lemonade in an old-school steel can a kid punctures with a church-key can opener strung to his belt loop.

Around sundown we pull into Kuala Lumpur and I stride into the Moorish-style main hall of KL station, which is also not seeing much traffic today. Good. No way can the sleepers be sold out.

"The sleepers are sold out," says the Malay ticket agent, without checking the manifest, then looks beyond me to the next person in line who's not there. "Departure at 21:30."

"*Terima kasih*," I thank him, for nothing. He brushes me aside like a gnat. In Indonesia my attempts at the native tongue were encouraged, endearing; here, evidently, they offend. An educated Malay expects to be recognized immediately as such and addressed in English.

Waiting for my connection I dine on street food. Service here is brisk and efficient. Chicken satay is served in a cone made from twisted-up pages torn from a phone book, smothered in peanut sauce and diced green onions. At another stand, ice-cubes bob tantalizingly in huge plastic urns filled with freshly squeezed tropical fruit juices: *Resist!* Ice is the devil. Very well then, a bottle of Tiger. There are times when a beer is the only safe choice.

Sated, I'm people-watching when some preteen boys approach. They're adorable, wearing in-style flower-print shirts with billowing sleeves and long pointy collars.

"Will you play us a song?" asks the smallest and cutest of the group, his hair cut in a little rockstar shag.

I unzip my case. "What would you like to hear?"

"Do you know the song about Muhammad Ali?"

"I do!" I can tell he wants to sing along. "Do you?"

He nods, shy and cute as can be, and together we sing how Ali float like a butterfly and sting like a bee.

When I tell them where I'm from they flip out.

"Chicago! *Home* of Muhammad Ali!" The people of Kuala Lumpur worship him; he'd fought a title bout here in June.

"And you know what else? I've *met* the Black Superman!"

This is true. The Champ is known to wander Chicago's streets like any regular guy. One night last summer, a couple girlfriends and I had encountered him, alone, looking in the window of a Gold Coast menswear store. We'd congratulated him on his recent victory, and he gently shook each of our hands.

THE 1930s DIESEL-BELCHER pulls out of KL with two empty sleeper cars and a Sikh conductor with a pleasant demeanor that conveys a certain willingness. I can feel it; this one's gonna play ball.

"Good evening, sir." I hand him the sheaf of documents and my passport. "Are there any sleeping berths available?"

Deferential nod. *Perhaps* I may upgrade to a berth, *for a fee*, payable directly to himself.

Three Malaysian dollars later I'm ensconced in my berth with the curtain closed and window open to admit the cool breeze and clackety-clack of wheels meeting track.

I love these sounds, the feel of the rock and sway, the world passing by out the window: ever since I was a little girl, riding the Duluth-Superior Limited to visit my grandparents in northern Wisconsin, for as far back as I can remember, I have always loved trains.

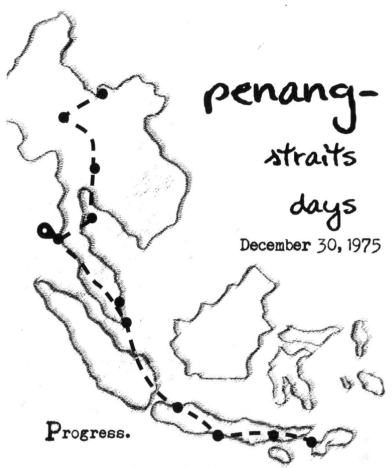

# penang–

## straits

## days

**December 30, 1975**

**Progress.**

Downtown George Town's narrow streets are paved. Bicycles and trishaws, motorcycles and buses proceed in an orderly fashion. Gone are the oxcarts and horse-drawn carriages of Java, the pounding rains. These streets are clean and dry. Tangled utility wires hang low overhead, just above the palms. These streets are lit at night.

A city of shabby Victorian buildings bleached white by the sun, of Hindu temples, Muslim mosques, and Christian churches, George Town is a monument to the country's colonial past and diverse population.

The Book suggests staying in George Town proper, devoting a scant, cautionary paragraph to Batu Ferringhi, the popular beach hangout up the coast. Immigration disapproves of hippie backpackers renting out rooms from the villagers, the authors report. To avoid trouble, stay away.

I'm thumbing through it for a hotel recommendation when a boy approaches.

"Hi lady. You look for the bus?"

I close The Book. "The bus to where?"

He lifts my suitcase. "Batu Ferringhi."


ON A QUIET, SHADY STRETCH along Penang's north coast, where jungle footpaths converge at Mama's café and general store, another boy is waiting. *Welcome!* He lifts my valise overhead, starts down a path towards the sound of waves crashing and turns, like Lassie leading Timmy home: *follow me.*

So I do. No young kid ever gave me a bum steer.

He leads me to a beachfront property, perched atop a ridge. From its porch I can observe the sights and sounds of the sea, the ebb and flow of the tide, the arrival and departure of the beach-goers and fishing boats, the whole circle of life in the village.

The landlady, Chinese, a seamstress, looks me up and down. Australian? American. She nods, quotes me five *ringgit* a night and her teenage daughter shows me around.

I'm given a corner bedroom, large and comfortable, with a window overlooking the Strait. The curtains drift, a fan twirls from the thatched-palm ceiling high overhead, cats and lizards scamper along the rafters. Outside, waves sweep the shore, crabs scuttle and wading birds peck in the tidal pools. The setting is peaceful and idyllic yet teeming with motion and life.

At dusk, on the porch, I watch the sun sink behind the hills and thank the travel gods who delivered me here.

That night I'm having Mama's house special *es kopi susu*, swirling sweetened-condensed milk from the bottom of the iced-coffee and licking it off the long-handled spoon, watching hunky Aussies slam Fosters, when a man in khaki shorts and wool knee socks raises his voice over the jukebox: *hallo, hallo*—a Brit—like he's tapping a microphone.

The Europeans look up at him, the Aussies at each other. *What the fuck,* one of them mutters.

"Conditions are ideal to view the bioluminescent plankton this evening," he announces, on the off-chance that someone will know what he's talking about.

"TREVOR!"

"As ever!" Last seen in Jogjakarta, the educator strides towards me, continuing to address the room. "This presents a rare opportunity to experience a remarkable phenomenon. WHO WOULD LIKE TO JOIN US?"

Nobody.

Trish turns to some guys creating a tower of beer cans. "Any of you dossers coming?"

Cowed by her teacher voice, none of them look up. A record drops on the jukebox. Merle Haggard is proud to be an Okie from Muskogee. The Aussies cheer and drink beer.

Trevor looks all around the room. "ANYBODY?" Among the adventurer-seekers there are no takers.

"Carry on then." One of Trevor's countrymen sweeps his arm towards the Strait, then returns to his Guinness.

"Not a very inquisitive lot, are they?" Trish, marching through a stand of sea oats. "They travel the earth, leaving a trail of wasted opportunities in their wake."

"Come now, dear," Trevor says. "Let us not be judgmental of those useless wankers."

I'd wasted a few opportunities myself. "How was Ubud?"

It was fascinating, exceptional, the highlight of their visit to Bali. Case in point: I'd never gotten there.

"People take to the road for different reasons." Trevor trains his flashlight on the ground, mindful of disturbing the early rising fishermen in their homes lining the shore.

"Some are running away—bad breakups, troubles on the job, family problems, what-have-you." He unties his hiking boots. "Others are working towards something. We've come to learn, to take this all back to our students."

"To bring the textbooks to life." Trish unties her sarong. "But enough on us. What brought you to this part of the world?"

I explain. A rare opportunity presented itself, just like tonight; I took advantage of it. I wasn't fleeing or anything.

"Not all of us are." Trevor unzips his fly.

"I'm just not sure...wait. We're going in? I thought you two hate sand."

Trevor ties his boots together. "Go on. You're not sure..."

"That's all. I'm not sure. It's kind of like, Meno's Paradox. 'How can one question that which one does not know...'"

"That's a bit circular, Yankee bird." Trevor steps out of his shorts.

"Exactly. That's why I majored in Philosophy. The final was always an essay test you could bullshit your way through. There were no wrong answers."

Trish says, "I always tell my students, 'there's no shame in not having the answers. The shame is in not asking the questions.'" She stacks their clothes at a safe distance from the tide. "Come along, luv." Her disembodied voice floats above the waves lapping and jungle sounds in the moonless night. "You have to disturb the planktons' environment to see them glow."

Trevor wades in and projects forward into the waves. His arms and legs create neon-blue swirls outlined against the night sky.

"Watch! Guess which stroke I'm doing," Trish calls. Plankton defining her limbs like an x-ray. She does the breaststroke, then the sidestroke, then two naked forms outlined in phosphorescent algae wade towards each in the gentle warm water, and I look away to give them a moment in the starry night.

WE GATHER AROUND SIX O'CLOCK, after the sun dips behind the hills along the northwest coast. We're a group of about 30, from Down Under and North America, Scandinavia and Germany, The Low Countries and France: we are Malaysian, Chinese, Indian, and British, assembled to celebrate New Year's Eve in island tradition—on the beach, around a fire.

One Malay guy digs a circular pit, places a steel garbage-can lid on the damp sand and loads it with chunks of dried-out driftwood. Another man strips bark off branches collected from nearby jungle scrub and inserts them crosswise in the cool, dense sand above the coals: the grill.

They barbecue chicken fresh from a roadside poultry farm, marinated in coconut milk and seasoned with the flavorings of Penang curry.

As daylight fades and the decibel level rises, the people start loosening up and the clothes start coming off. Europeans, Aussies and New Zealanders and Californians go charging into the surf, butts and boobs bouncing, while I remain clothed and ashore among the British, the Canadians, the men of color who don't go in for this sort of thing.

I love the ocean. I love walking along the shore, listening to the surf pound and the gulls cry; inhaling the fresh sea air, gazing across the sea to beyond the horizon, all this is fine.

But nothing about plunging naked amongst strangers into bath-temperature saltwater teeming with micro-organisms strikes me as a good idea. I was imprinted on the fresh, sweet, cool waters of Lake Michigan, that are not harmful when swallowed.

*"Allo!"* One of the Europeans is loping towards me with his hand outstretched. *"I am Zhoo-weesh too!"* Impressive. I have to come within arms' length, whereas this *Landsmann* has picked me off at 50 paces. His accent is adorable and so is he, with shiny black ringlets, luminous dark eyes and a proud Hebrew profile: the classic good-looking Jewish boy.

I introduce myself that way we do, by first name and hometown.

"Ah yess! The girl from Che-cah-go! My name is Jack. But not really." He flips open a passport lettered in Cyrillic picturing a Jack Somebody who is dark, but not tall, and not handsome.

"Black market passport." He strokes his moustache. "I get in a leetle trouble—drug bust. My passport was...eh... con-fees-cated."

"Rather a shitty likeness." Peering over my shoulder and reeking of Guinness is the Brit who'd summarily dismissed Trevor and his plankton last night. "Why, hel-*lo*." He tips his bottle towards me. "From whence do you hail?"

I'm like, "Whence? Come on. Who talks like that?"

"I do! Particularly when pissed." He casts bleary eyes at his wrist. He's not wearing a watch. "We began at 10:45 AM sharp, continuing throughout the day, except for a brief interruption during the afternoon when some Yankee bird— they said she was from Chicago—came cycling up to Mama's with a police escort. We figgered it was *Immigrasi*, starting up one of their infamous Hippie Clearances on New Year's Eve." The Brit stifles a belch. "Now where did you say you're from?"

"Chicago."

He attempts to focus on me. "Bloody. Fucking. Hell. You. YOU? I almost SHAT myself!"

I explain that I'm sorry, I didn't know about the Clearances. "But what's the problem, if your visa's not expired?"

"That's not the *iss-you!*" His diction is excellent for someone this drunk. "They're looking for Westerners renting rooms from the villagers! If you're not staying in a licensed lodging, they have grounds to expel you. Evidently. So where are you staying?"

I point to my Chinese landlady's house on the ridge about 150 yards back, with its veranda overlooking the beach.

"A private home? You could be deported, you know."

"What a bunch of bullshit."

A skinny Yank in knee-length white Indian tunic and elephant bell-bottoms who appears not to have changed clothes in six years has wandered up. He has a scraggly beard, long, stringy hair and did not chip in for the food and beer.

"Visas, deportation, borders. What bullshit. We're citizens of the WORLD. These artificial boundaries are *so* fucked. In Kathmandu in '72, we all tore up our passports and proclaimed ourselves citizens of Freak. Fuckin.' Alley!"

Jack-Not-Really rolls his eyes at me. "*Oy.* A *meshuggeneh.* See you lay-terre."

"We were there for months, no hassles," Freak Dude continues. No one responds. "Now there's all these rules, the three little visa pictures, all those stamps. Fuckin' bureaucracy. It's just not like it was. You guys?" With a sweep of the hand, he indicates the assembled group. "You all missed out."

The drunken Brit bites. "I beg your pardon. This 'fuckin' bureaucracy' represents the dying vestiges of our late, great Empire." He raises his beer. "Let her sun never set!"

"That is truly fucked. A toast to like, rampant imperialism."

The Brit turns on the hippie-dippie. "Taking ourselves a little, seriously, are we? It's New Year's Eve, for God's sake. Rampant imperialism." He lurches away, muttering.

"And HERE!" So now I'm stuck with him. "This place is the worst. These fucking Clearances! I heard *Immigrasi* raided Mama's this afternoon! On New Year's Eve!"

"It wasn't a raid. It was just this one nice guy giving me a ride. He didn't bust anybody."

The throwback stiffens. "So *you're* the one who brought Immigration to Mama's?"

"It wasn't Immigration."

"Oh FUCK." He looks around, decides he has crashed the wrong party and heads down the beach.

The Brit circles back with a fresh drink. "Cheers. You got rid of that tosser?"

"He left."

"Good-o. NO MORE CLEARANCES! Say. I'll bet you don't know the derivation of that expression."

A Nordic type says, "I believe it's a word play on 'Highland Clearances,' when the English drove the Scottish clans off their land and seized their ancestral homes..."

"Absolutely correct!" The Brit extends his hand. "Simon of Chester. You are a very..."— he sways a bit— "learned fellow. I admire that. As Churchill stated: 'those who do not study history are doomed to repeat it.'"

"Magnus. Copenhagen." He shakes Simon's hand. "Churchill didn't state that. He was quoting it."

"Why do the British get such a bad rap?" I interject. "They invested in their colonies. Built roads and bridges, schools, basic services..."

"Like the Romans!" Simon says.

Magnus raises an eyebrow. "You realize their motives weren't altruistic. These countries gave up their land, their sovereignty..."

"Well, I...yeah."

"It went beyond simple conquest," Magnus says. "England sought to make the world over in its own image."

"That's extremely insightful!" Simon belches admiringly.

"What were you doing with that cop, anyways?" asks a guy with scraggly blond hair and gold John Lennon wire rims. "Steve," he says. "Toronto."

"He wasn't a cop, he was in the militia. He offered me a lift downtown. He gave me his helmet. He was just a nice guy."

"Yes, they all are," says Steve. "Very nice. To the CHICKS!" He looks around at the handful of women at the party.

He'd transported me to the bank, then the Botanic Garden, a city park with streams and waterfalls.

"Dozens of chimps, just roaming free. Incredible."

"Chimps are apes," an Indian guy says. "Those were probably rhesus macaques. Did they have tails?"

"Macaques, whatever. Wandering all over. And they weren't so friendly. This one grabs a bag of grapes out of my hand, goes and sits on a rock, staring at me, spitting out the seeds. What an asshole! They were kinda sour anyway."

"Must've been the alpha male," an American girl says.

"I know, right?" The monkeys, I don't mention, had been getting it on right and left. Militia Guy, fortunately, was waiting in the parking lot, reading the paper while all this was going on.

"So he drops me off at Mama's afterwards and everyone's screaming. '*IMMIGRASI! IMMIGRASI!*'" I wave my arms. "Running out the back door! It was a riot!"

"Hilarious," Simon says. "I almost shat myself." Later he'll pass out under the palm tree my guitar is leaning against.

New Year's Eve is clear and moonless. The stars begin to rise, more than I've seen since those summers in Superior. "*Look kids!*" *Daddy points to a huge white cloud full of stars, like a band of shiny dust. "You can see the Milky Way!"*

"Hey, Chicago!" an Aussie yells. "You gonna play that guitar?"

Deep breath. "YEAH, I'M GONNA PLAY."

"*Daddy, what makes thunder?*" *He turns from pushing the mower. "Thunder is God's kids running to see him when he gets home from work." When was that? Must've been the summer before.*

Swallow hard. "YOU GUYS GONNA SING?"

So I strum and I sing, I fight back like I always do, because we all know *You can't. Always. Get. What you want! You can't. Always. Get. What you want!*

And they all join in. They always do.

As midnight approaches, I think about my friends celebrating New Year's Eve on this frigid night back home— the girls forgetting their gloves in bars, the guys jump-starting their cars—and suddenly I'm groping on the blankets, frantic to leave. "Anyone see a flashlight?"

"They call them torches," an American says.

Jack-Not-Really intercepts me on the way up the ridge.

"I carry zees." He reaches for my guitar. "So. You have enough of ze party?"

"I just kind of wanted to be alone at midnight."

He nods. "Homesick?"

"Guess so. How 'bout you?"

He stops walking. "*Non.* I left home at the age of *feef-teen.* I do not miss it."

"Where's home? You're French, right?"

"Belgian. But not really."

Then we're on my porch. Jack leaning against the railing, tree frogs chirping; the skunky aroma of fresh bud.

His parents had managed to outrun the Nazis. They'd been sent to Belgium after the war, DPs, and settled there to raise Jack and his sister. But he hadn't stuck around.

"So where you headed next?" I pass him the corncob.

"Next? I go north, cross into Thailand..."

The Malay-Thai border is infamous. Assholes at Immigration, backpacks getting searched, it's scary enough crossing clean, let alone with a black-market passport and prior drug bust: the same risk he'll face at every border.

Jack correctly interprets my silence. "No worries. Remember, I am the son of Survivors. I will make it home."

And so he will. Months later, on a cold, drizzly Athens morning, crossing Syntagma Square, I'll hear someone pounding on the window of the American Express office. Jack will come bursting out and we'll embrace like the long-lost relatives we sort of were. *Thank God you made it*, I'll say, *want to go for coffee or something?*

And he'll say *non*, he can't give up his place in line, but he saw that guitar going past and had to come out. He'll rest a hand on my shoulder and say, I knew I would see you again, and I'll think, *really? I didn't*. Then I'll take his picture, so I'll always have a shot of Jack-Not-Really to remember him by.

But right now all I know is I want to go in. "It's almost midnight."

Jack takes the hint. "I go to Mama's. «*Bonne année*.»"

"Happy New Year. Wait. What's your real name?"

He leans down. "It's Abner," he whispers. He seems sad to have given up his identity. Then he straightens up. "But call me Jack. I mus' get yoose to *eet*."

When he's gone I tune in the midnight countdown on the BBC. Everybody I know is surrounded by people they know, everybody I love is with someone they love, and now I am engulfed. Homesickness drags me along in its undertow: *the road it gets lonely*, that voice in my head sings—but then I surface. I poke my head out the window and hear the surf pounding, the partygoers reveling and I'm happy once again to be just where I am—having the adventure of a lifetime on the other side of the world.

NEW YEAR'S MORNING at Mama's I'm poring over someone's left-behind, week-old Straits Times when an American voice asks if I ever found my flashlight.

I look up and close the paper. "Just in time. Made it back before 12. Lin, from Berkeley, right?"

"Right." She sits down. "That's around when I left. I kind of wanted to be by myself at midnight."

"Me too! I listened to Auld Lang Syne on the BBC."

"Not *too* sentimental." And just like that she's got my number, has seen beneath my hard-shell exterior to the secret, liquid core.

Lin is 26, the adorable girl-next-door, with blonde Orphan Annie ringlets, big blue eyes, freckles and deep dimples. A faded sarong tied over one shoulder drapes her slim frame. She's the real deal: A Traveling Woman; took off after college.

"You've been on the road for four years? Holy crap."

She smokes Dunhills, hard to come by. "Have one. My boyfriend brings them from Singapore." He works for an American company, she explains, running an oil platform on the South China Sea. "Mike's from Texas, they figured he knows oil. He's coming this weekend, he couldn't get off for New Year's..."

"I just came from Singapore. Wait. He's from Texas and you're from Berkeley. You met on the ROAD?"

"In Goa. We've been together the whole time."

"Wow." Every backpacker girl's secret fantasy is to meet The One on The Road.

"So, Lin." I stub out the Dunhill. "Those fancy resorts that next town over. You up for a little jaunt?"

We manage to sneak into a locker room, scrub and shampoo luxuriously in the hot showers, but when we take a couple chairs at the pool the jig is up.

"Those guys are pointing at us," Lin says. We start walking. So do the two attendants.

We turn towards the beach. They follow.

SHIT! We chorus. We dash from the pool onto the blistering sand where they won't likely give chase.

"Goddammit! We just took a shower. Already I'm sweating."

"My FEET!" Lin springs towards the damp, cool, hard-packed sand at water's edge. "Over here. The tide is out." Barefoot we trudge along the beach to whence we came, then up the ridge to my house, sand flies nipping at our ankles.

"Wanna cool off at my place, have a few hits?" I fan myself with my tee-shirt.

"Sure. Hey! There's that French guy on your porch."

"Jack? He's Belgian. But not really."

LATER AT MAMA'S, the men who sit around drinking all day have been sitting around and drinking all day, and they have grown surly.

"Fuckin' Yanks! The U.S should be supplying more foreign aid to the Third World!" one of them shouts in our direction.

*Yeah, fuckin' Yanks,* the others grumble into their beer mugs.

I turn from the counter where we're placing our orders. Lin shakes her head: *Don't bother.* Jack gives me a look: *zey are idiotes.* But I have never been able to resist a loud public disagreement with a misinformed stranger.

"More foreign aid?" I walk over to their table. "Disasters. Famines. Epidemics. Whatever. Who's first on the scene? The United States of America."

"Oh, that's humanitarian aid. I'm talking about ECONOMIC STIMULUS. For countries who need"—he wags an unsteady finger in my face—"to pave their roads. Mend their bridges. That sort of thing." He tips his chair back and folds his arms across his chest.

"Well guess what?" I lean in. "We have bad roads. Our bridges are caving in. The El train I live right next to is crumbling. Are we supposed to put everyone else's needs ahead of our own?"

"That's very selfish," says another Aussie. "With all your resources…"

I turn on him. "You're from a wealthy country. How much aid does Australia send? To its neighbors right here in Southeast Asia?"

"Our economy is no match for yours," he snaps, like this lets them off the hook.

"Of course not!" Now Lin's had it. "You have to support your welfare state! All those people lying around on the dole!"

Ten months of continuous employment qualifies Aussies for unemployment compensation that never seems to expire. They have it wired from home, basically a subsidy to smoke cigarettes, drink beer and pick fights all day with the rest of us who worked and saved to get here.

"I waitressed in Darwin," Lin says. "They were thrilled to hire me. You know why? Because Yanks *hustle*. That's what my boss said. He liked my Yankee work ethic."

"He liked your Yankee ass," another guy says, which is obnoxious but cuts the tension somewhat.

"What *I* hate about Yanks," he continues, "is how you're so clannish. Always— sticking together."

"Yeah, 'cause everyone else hates us."

"That's not it. It's like some fuckin'...magnetic force. The minute you meet, you're best friends. *'Whereya from? Whereya from?'* He mocks our accents with precision. "Across a room, above people's heads, you're always yelling to each other." He belches, the man lecturing me about manners. "You're very LOUD people."

"And when you get up from the table, you do not push your chairs back in!" cries someone nearby in an obscure Middle European accent. He'd never spoken before and he never does again.

Jack drifts over to the Europeans surrounding the jukebox, speaking to each in his mother tongue; our orders come, the tables fill up, the place gets noisy; the dying embers of our debate with the angry Aussies are snuffed out.

When Lin and I get up to leave for sunset Jack snaps to attention. He has a highly developed sixth sense that alerts him when someone else's pot is about to be smoked.

"Hold it a minute," I say. "Wait'll he's not looking." Jack's a sweet guy, but he stifles the girl talk; also, he's making a hell of a dent in my stash.

We give him the slip and go to the beach, passing wooden racks where thousands of tiny shrimps have been laid out to dry, stinking to high heaven.

"They grind these into shrimp paste," Lin says. "Boy, what assholes!"

"I shouldn't have started with them. But thanks for the back up."

We go on a riff about how travel has made us appreciate our native land. Democracy, free enterprise, lots of free stuff: matchbooks, coffee refills, bread and butter at restaurants. Clean public restrooms, safe drinking fountains, freedom of the press. The list is long and Yanks never tire of reciting and adding to it: Things We Took for Granted.

We take off our sandals and pad over to the cooler, denser sand. A lot has changed in the four years Lin's been gone, I tell her. Women's Lib, the Equal Rights Amendment. There's been a bit of backlash. Male-female relations are in flux. Sex has gone from spiritual to casual, guys from sensitive to macho; everyone's confused. "So now we're expected to pay our own way on dates *and* put out. You're lucky, you've missed all this crap over here in Asia."

She smiles. Lucky? "Wait'll you meet him."

We hang out on the beach past sunset, till the streaks of pink and orange surrender to purple and magenta, then blue-black, the color of my favorite crayon, the color of Van Gogh's Starry Night. The constellations rise.

Lin tells me stories, according to the oral tradition of the Trail. She'd graduated from UC Berkeley, then gone to London to ride the Magic Bus. From Athens to Istanbul, she'd wandered East, sometimes solo, sometimes not.

Alone in Kabul, she'd been pestered and pawed to such extremes she disguised herself as a boy for a week. That didn't work. "That culture is so repressive, there's a prison mentality. They go for boys—blonds, especially."

Lin and I discover we have more in common than just being two Yank girls in the same place. Both daughters of physicians, we both stayed home for college, we're both political and social liberals with certain traditional values: marriage, fine; husband being the major breadwinner, fine.

"I think taking the guy's last name is fine," I say. "But then I hate my last name. It's..." I take a deep breath. "It's not my real name, anyway."

Waves are lapping gently at the shore; the tide has gone out. She looks at me: *go on.*

"My father died when I was six. My brother and I were getting over the mumps. My mom was pregnant."

*Mommy and Gramma crying in the front room, where no one ever sat. Mommy has a handkerchief over her face.*

*"What's wrong?" I ask. They don't answer. "Is Daddy d-e-d?" I sound it out, just like in school.*

*Mommy looks at me like she's surprised. Then she covers her eyes with the handkerchief again and nods.*

"Do you remember him?" Lin asks.

"I do. Especially now. Since I've been traveling. It's like all these memories have been unearthed." *Daddy taking pictures, making movies with his cameras; Daddy fishing, playing softball, skiing, playing guitar, hammering wood, listening to records, reading books, writing stories, building model trains. Daddy loved trains.* "He was brilliant. A lawyer."

Then I tell her the happy stuff: my sister being born a couple months later, my mother meeting a high-school girlfriend's older brother, by then an eligible doctor, their whirlwind courtship and marriage, our stepdad adopting us and bringing us into a loving new family with the tease-inducing name which, it turns out, wasn't theirs either, but the name of whoever met their grandfather at Ellis Island.

We carry our sandals back up the ridge, and Lin asks how old my father was, and what he died of.

"Thirty-seven," I say. "Juvenile diabetes."

She stops walking. "That's hereditary."

"Yeah. None of us got it."

THE NEXT DAY I wander over to the commercial docks where fishermen are hauling in their catch. A couple backpackers I take for Aussies are watching the men work the nets.

One has a receding hairline with long scraggly locks down his neck. The other has shaggy brown hair streaked red-dish gold by the sun, the exact same color as mine. As I approach, he turns to catch my eye.

I am caught.

He's in a khaki work shirt, sleeves rolled to mid-forearm, and in the cooler-than-usual weather, we are wearing identical, out-of-style, straight-leg Levis. He asks if I speak English: *American.*

"You really can't tell?" I am so obviously who I am; no one ever asks.

Waves lapping at the shore, cuttlefish wriggling in the nets, men shouting to each other in Malay, his eyes the color of the sea: he smiles.

"Didn't want to presume." He extends his hand. "I'm Peter. This is Ernie."

They're from Santa Barbara, firefighters for the Fed who'd won open-ended round-trip fares to Bangkok for their outstanding performance during wildfire season.

They walk back with me to town, up and over the dunes, the conversation meandering with the path. Why'd you quit your job and come traveling? he asks.

I explain. The visit to Tokyo that set me on this course; the subsequent stumble upon the Hippie Trail.

"So we're all here kind of by happenstance," Peter says. And he's making the most of it, filming a documentary in pursuit of a master's degree in journalism. "What about you? Are you working on something here?"

I bend down and turn up my pants cuffs. "I play guitar. I write songs. Also I just, you know. Write." I tell the sand.

"Pardon? You're a songwriter? Maybe we could hear you play later."

In contrast with his macho occupation and physique, Peter has a boyish, almost childlike fascination for everything he sees and hears. He's an intent listener, a prodder who makes you feel like your every comment is thought-provoking, important, worthy of a considered response, or challenge. He revels in words. Just like me.

We're bumping shoulders, carrying our shoes, Ernie a couple steps to the side. Crabs scuttle through tidal pools fiery with the reflection of the setting sun, wading birds peck at the sand; we've been talking and walking for hours.

A wave washes over our feet and we watch it foam. "You guys hungry?" Peter looks from me to Ernie.

We watch sunset, have dinner, we kick back on the porch and I play for them, putting the guitar, and then myself, in open tuning, just tripping up and down the frets, waiting to see what's going to come next.

Next day, we're pedaling rented bikes all over the island, Peter and Ernie and an addition to the squad, Hari, an Indian college student on semester break they met at their guesthouse.

Nineteen and nice looking, wearing a white short-sleeved button-down, black chinos and black wingtips and riding a Hot Wheels, Hari will be going back to university with some great stories for his buddies.

We wind up deserted roads through the rain forests dense with rubber trees, humongous, the way they look in real life, not someone's living room, dripping what looks like Elmer's Glue into huge buckets it takes two men to carry, suspended from a pole across their shoulders.

Taking single steps to control the sloshing, they inch their way to a pickup, upend their load into a storage cylinder and return to milk the tree again, just like one of those Bell Telephone movies you used to see in 5th grade: does Peter remember those?

Not only does he remember, he was one of the boys who got to wheel in the projector.

"You were in AV club?"

"What, you've pegged me as an AV club nerd?"

I swerve towards him. "I was in orchestra. I played viola. I was like, the nerd of nerds."

He swerves back and we smile at each other. *Look how cool we both turned out.*

The road summits in a secluded section of forest where graduated pools spill into one another in dappled sunlight.

Entranced, Peter walks around taking photos from various angles, then hands me his camera, strips naked, lowers into one of the pools and tells me to take his picture. "It's focused, just press the shutter."

I heft his camera like, oh sure, this is totally normal, keeping my eyes trained resolutely north.

"This is great." He spreads his arms. "You coming in?"

Ernie drops trow and submerges, Hari stammers something about public nudity being frowned upon in Muslim countries and stands guard at the street, and suddenly I'm shedding my outer attire and inner viola and darting into a shaded pool in water up to my chin.

Peter gets some shots with his camera, Ernie with mine. When my film is developed nothing is revealed, but I'll wonder what Peter's professional-grade equipment recorded of this little adventure.

We return the bikes, watch the sunset, pass the corncob, the four of us. Hari doesn't inhale. We have dinner, the three of us. Ernie sticks around. They see me home, both of them: it's very dark and I'm not wearing my glasses because they make me look like a dork, so I can't see a thing and end up flopping into a sand-pit neck-deep and looking way dorkier.

"Ohmigod. You OK?" Peter pulls me out, with warm, strong, callused man-hands. "Gee. You're kind of a clutz."

We're looking at each other, laughing, He's holding my hands. He's *still* holding my hands...

"Sure you're OK?" Ernie asks.

Oh. Yeah. He's still here. In a perfect world, he wouldn't be, but it's like the song says. You can't always get what you want.

But sometimes...the next morning only Peter is waiting at Mama's.

He looks me up and down in my new custom-tailored flour sack ensemble—cut a bit too form-fittingly, I thought—wiggles his eyebrows, leans excitingly close and says, "There's a Hindu temple I want to shoot a little ways uphill."

What *is* it with this guy? We've spent every waking moment together since we met, told each other our life stories, even skinny-dipped, and the whole time he's maintained this earnest, sincere, Boy Scout demeanor while I've been harboring impure thoughts about how nicely he fills out those Levi 505s.

Hindu temples are never a little ways uphill. It's a morning's exertion; when we finally get there he climbs around, shooting photos while I wait in a torturous line snaking all the way down the rocky incline to the entrance.

Too long later he rescues me from this line and the conversation I've been having with an Indian couple.

"What was all that about? I was watching. That girl didn't like you talking to her boyfriend."

"We were talking politics. Why should she care?"

"She did. And the interesting thing was, you weren't picking up on it. At all." He has this good-natured way of chiding me—of showing that he's on to my foibles and quirks, but maybe does not mind them.

In the afternoon we rent a sailboat from one of the resorts. He shows me how to sit, some ropes to pull, and somehow I manage to keep the sail full and the boat going forward.

"That's right! You have to kind of anticipate the wind. Gee! You're a natural."

I turn to acknowledge the compliment and he leans closer. *Ohmigod*, is he gonna..

"You look like my ex-wife." The boat starts circling. "You have to work the rudder while the sails are full, so you can..."

"Ex-wife?"

"I was married in college." We listen to the sails flap.

"I was too." I tell him he also reminds me of someone. "Not a real person though." *I sound like a smitten teenager.* "Finny. In *A Separate Peace.* Have you read it?"

"I have." He doesn't sound warm to the comparison.

Then the wind dies, and he has to get us back before we're charged for another half hour, so there's no more talk of college marriages or high school crushes.

Afterwards we hang around the pool, among the honeymooners, families and empty-nesters on holiday for a week, not a year, all dressed up, carrying shopping bags: it's hard to imagine we're all occupying the same dimension, the same space and time.

That night we have dinner with Lin and her boyfriend Mike, a major hunk.

"We're starving." Lin has stars in her eyes that leave little doubt as to how they'd worked up such an appetite.

Peter passes me the menu. "We are too. Did we actually ever eat today?"

*We.* Like it's a real double-date, at a real cafe, where the lights twinkle and the bottles are cold enough to sweat.

"Purty soon, we're leavin' this all behind." Mike rests his big man-hand on Lin's forearm. "Time for that next phase. Gonna build us a house in the country."

"Mike's house," she says. "That he designed. He drew up blueprints."

"Kentucky, mebbe. Real pretty country. Affordable. Away from the rat race. Nice place to raise a family."

Lin smiles wide, her dimples deepening.

"Kentucky *is* beautiful in parts," Peter agrees. "Or Virginia. That's where I'm originally from."

This is news. "You're not a native Californian?"

"No. My father got transferred a lot. I've been there a long time, though. Majored in Film at UC Santa Barbara."

"The nicest town in Southern California," Lin says.

Peter picks up on the little dig. "You must be from up north."

"Berkeley. Born and raised."

He nods. "I might end up there for grad school. I'm working on my application while I'm here. What do you guys know about the situation in Burma?"

We know what most Overlanders know. You can only get a 7-day visa, are required to fly between prescribed destinations, as ground travel is forbidden, and supposedly the entire week's travel can be bankrolled by the sale of a smuggled carton of Marlboros.

"Their asshole dictator Ne Win has closed the country down," Peter says. "Foreign goods only come through the black market. There's civil war. The minority Karen are fighting the Burmans for self-rule." He accents the last syllable: Ka-REN.

"I've made contact with the rebel force—the KNLA—to film a documentary. I start shooting when I get back to Bangkok."

Later I'll wonder how a 26-year-old kid from Santa Barbara got embedded with the Karen National Liberation Army. But there and then, I'm struck by how concrete, how doable these plans all sound; grad school, buying a house, whereas mine are such a pipe dream.

I tell them about being turned down for a promotion due to lack of experience, only to learn the station GM's son got the job straight out of college, with no experience.

"Nepotism, what bullshit," Peter says. "So now?"

"So now. I'm thinkin' about...trying to make a go playing music. Well, writing songs. For someone who can *really* sing."

I'm under no illusions that my voice is headline material. I'll be content to sing back up, play rhythm guitar. Write the songs. Call the shots.

After dinner—which Mike insists on paying for because he earns American wages and has no living expenses—Peter has to go to his place to pack.

"I'll meet up with you all in a little while. Thanks for dinner, man." He and Mike shake hands, the Boy Scout and the cowboy.

After that the three of us go hang out at my place and listen to the waves.

"Mike's a Texas boy," Lin says. "He can yodel." "Texans? Yodel?"

"Yep. That's how we call the cattle." He nods at the guitar. "You play any country? Slim Whitman?"

Never heard of him. Country music: three simple chords. "I can fake it."

He starts out in a rich baritone and vaults in and out of falsetto, just like on Lawrence Welk—who knew yodeling could be so sexy? I manage to tune in the Far East Network. We listen for a while.

We pass the pipe. We wait for Peter. Finally we get restless and walk back into town so we  don't connect with him again.


Around midnight I find him waiting on my porch. He says he was just about to leave, but he didn't wanna take off without... *without what?*

"Here's the number of the Karen house in Bangkok." He's all organized and efficient. "Call me when you get there. And here's my home address, so we can send each other pictures when we get back."

He asks me to tell Mike and Lin goodbye for him. We'd hung out as a foursome for just one night, but this is how it is on the road. The relationships are so accelerated, our emotions so intensified, it's like old, dear friends parting.

Then he says, can I have a hug?

We put our arms around each other. He's the perfect height for me, tall enough to look up to, but not so tall as to require my standing on tiptoe if we were to kiss, which, if not now, is probably going to be never.

I look up and he looks down, our lips cling softly for an instant longer than might be considered merely friendly, then he says he'd better get going.

"Be careful," I say. "Safe travels."

He chucks me under the chin. "See you in Bangkok."

Hari is waiting at Mama's the next morning with an envelope. "Peter wanted me to give you this." He seems pleased to play a role in our little melodrama.

Inside there's a sheet of notebook paper ripped from a spiral pad and folded in quarters. He's written me a poem.

As I find much of poetry, the language is musical but the meaning obscure. For the most part. A couple words are absent of any nuance: *Hunger. Fever.* This I get: that he's hungry, he's feverish, and he's leaving now.

The last two lines I will never understand and always remember.

*Your spit of polish, my bits of glass ~*
*In the mine of magic time*

MY HIGH SCHOOL CRUSH GOES TO BANGKOK to shoot his film, Mike and Lin go MIA, and I obsess about money. Thailand, Burma, Nepal, India. Israel. I'll have no money left for Europe. I fill pages with calculations and alternate itineraries, the girl who's going with the flow.

When my head's about to explode I take a break at Mama's, where Toronto Steve from New Year's Eve waves me over to meet two Yanks I take as a couple.

"Berenice—Joisey," she says. The guy tips his straw fedora. "Bill. Nebraska. Zepplin'?"

"Zepplin'?" That's kinda cute, and so is Bill, with short dark hair brushed straight back and neat black beard. "Is that what they say in Nebraska?"

"Nah, my buddy made it up. Got sick of S'happenin? So whehya from?"

The fedora, the dropped *r*, this guy's not from no Nebraska. "Chicago. So whereya originally from?"

Cute smile. "Flushing Meadows, New Yawk, site of the nineteen sixty-faw World's Fair."

"You're from Queens. And you moved to...where in Nebraksa?"

"Lincoln," he says. But not why.

"We're on our way to my place," Steve says. "For something special from Surabaya. You in?"

"Wur y'all goan?" We all look up. "Howdy," says Mike.

They're back. Things are officially looking up. I thought I'd lost them.

"Oooh!" Bill cocks his head. "A Texan! Whereabouts?"

"Lubbock. Mike. You?"

"Bill. Nebraska."

I look at Lin. "But not really."


Steve lives under someone's house.

Off the road, back in the jungle, it's staked up on pilings just high enough to let you sit up straight underneath. There's a plank floor and everything's enclosed in plywood.

He switches on a bare light bulb as we take turns crawling in. "Even got power down here. Great, huh? Cheap as camping, but better shelter than a tent."

Steve loves this little hobbit hole. Such low-cost accommodations free up funds for other things, such as— he unwraps a small tin-foil packet containing a tarry black chunk of goop—"Opium."

"How do you take it?" Bill asks. "In a pipe?"

"We can use my skag spoon." Steve fingers a small spoon hanging from a chain around his neck.

"What's a skag spoon?" I chirp.

Everyone exchanges uncomfortable glances.

"Skag means heroin," Steve finally mutters.

107

"Wow. Maybe it's cool to walk around wearing that in Toronto," says Lin, in a tone that conveys just about how cool *she* thinks it is. "Here, you're just asking for trouble."

Bill runs a hand over his close-cropped hair. "I'm not lookin' for trouble. Whacked off my hair. Used to be down to here." He points to the middle of his back. "Gotta say, it's great not having it all hanging down in this heat."

"Looks great, man," Mike says. Everybody laughs. Their haircuts are identical.

This is the great debate of the mid-70s—to cut or not to cut. To shave or not to shave. To grow up or remain a flower child.

Opium voted down, Steve's searching his stash for some hash when a storm swoops in and Berenice starts whining. "It's very stuffy down he-ah."

Nobody answers. Rain pounding all around us, runoff coursing through the sand, keeping dry is the main thing.

"Couldja crack open that trap daw?" She's hyperventilating now.

"Shit, it's a downpour." Steve starts stacking his gear on a wooden crate.

Visions of washed-out camping trips and flooded basements come to mind. "It's gonna start coming up through the floorboards pretty soon," I muse.

Mike looks just above his head at the tangle of colored wires stapled to the floor joists. "Wonder where this electric's runnin' in from? I don't think this wiring's up to code."

"Let me OUT OF HERE!" Berenice screeches.

Steve crumbles some hash into a pipe. "Maybe wait a bit till it subsides?"

"NO!" She crawls over our legs and fumbles with the latch, pounding on the door, screaming "Open this, GODDAMNIT," then scuttles out and bolts to the road in the hammering rain.

Evidently she and Bill weren't an item. Nobody knows where she runs off to, and we never see her again.

Bill and I just kind of fall in together over the next couple days. Things are easy between us. I don't wonder whether he likes me or get the shivers when he looks at me. He's like the guys I hung around with in college.

He majored in psych, played bass guitar in a rock band, graduated and went to work at a state mental hospital, an identical trajectory to several guys I knew, including my brother. We're comfortable together, running errands, sharing observations, finding analogies to Star Trek in our daily lives: like on the bus.

You buy a ticket from the driver, then present it to a uniformed female attendant; she inspects it, tears it in half, then sweeps her arm towards the empty seats. Only then may we be seated; no sweep, no sit.

"Boy," says Bill. "Patronage out the yin-yang."

"I know, right? It's as though they've elevated the British bureaucracy to an art form. Like that highly imitative culture the Enterprise discovered on..."

"Sigma Iotia II! With the gangsters? I love that one!"

In Bill I've found a buddy who can recite episodes line by line. Someone to sing and talk and joke and smoke with. So this is how we pass the next few days.


THE FRIDAY BEFORE my visa expires, Lin and I, Steve and Bill are at the beach while I obsessively tune my guitar and fret about Bangkok.

"It's not as bad as they say," Lin says. "You'll be fine."

"It's in tune," says Bill. "Stop already. Where's the lighter?"

I pass him my Zippo.

"I'm scared I'll get ripped off. The crime, the heat, the filth."

"Hot showers, air-conditioning, flush toilets," Lin counters.

Fair-skinned Steve is starting to fry. "I gotta get into some shade. Wanna come back to my place?"

"Nah." Bill looks at me. "Let's go to our house."

Lin and Steve look back and forth. 'Our' house?

"Bill's staying at my place now." I let them speculate as to exactly where.

We start up the dune. I'm resigned. My visa's almost up, my train ticket's already booked. I leave on Monday as planned.

Or not.

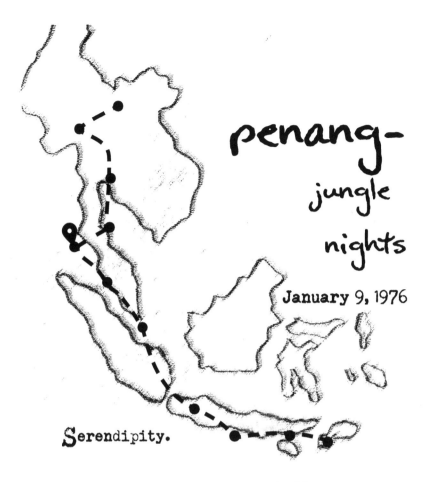

penang-
jungle
nights

January 9, 1976

Serendipity.

"What kind of music do you play?"

He's out of breath, tall and husky by Malay standards, well-dressed, with lustrous dark rock star hair, and a complexion of *kopi-susu*.

"Is that a set? May I see?" He's noticed the play list taped into the curve of my guitar. "An eclectic! Classic R&B, folk, rock, blues...I know all of this material. Except..." he points to the last song on the list. "This one."

"That's an original," I mumble.

He taps a British Oval against a gold cigarette case.

"I'm a lead singer. Would you like to run through a few songs? Where are you all off to right now?"

I gesture up the ridge.

"After you." He extends his hand. "I'm Allan."

Allan leans against the porch railing, framed in late afternoon light, and brings it on home. Song after song. He has a lower register of rich, dark chocolate and a soaring tenor range that carries the final sweet, high note of *Let It Be* over the ridge, to float above the waves.

"Tide's coming in," Bill murmurs, then we're all quiet again, under Allan's spell.

He gazes pensively out to the horizon, then turns to us and we lean forward, expecting some mystical, Eastern utterance.

"I can get us a gig tonight." He snaps his fingers.

That night we open at the Bamboo Din.

It's literally off-the-beaten-path, in a jungle clearing. Lantern-lit rattan tables and chairs on an open-air deck, a bar under a thatched-palm roof strung with twinkling lights, an audience of mostly middle-aged Aussies tourists seeking a more exotic setting than their resort dining room.

Allan loves to perform, but even more, he loves bringing disparate people together, stirring in some music and alcohol and seeing what develops.

The tourists are curious about us, and particularly fascinated by Toronto Steve, who sleeps in a crawl space.

"Why don't you cut your hair?" one of the ladies asks.

"This is cut," he says. "You should've seen it before!"

"Keep cutting."

The music flows effortlessly. Allan sings lead and Bill and I backup: *Under the Boardwalk, Cry to Me, Baby It's You.*

We switch leads. I do *Walkin' the Dog*, then something pretty, by the Beau Brummels: *Just a Little,* where you cry just a little and die just a little and have to go away. I love sad songs.

"Keep going," Allan says. "Your call."

Now in full sentimental mode, I choose an Israeli love song my Tokyo hosts had always played: *Erev Shel Shoshanim*— Night of Roses.

"Beautiful," Allan says afterwards. "That language was...?"

"Hebrew."

He smiles. "Teach it to me."

For a week we're the toast of the town.

Allan gets us in at Spaniards, a George Town club popular with the international crowd, where we enjoy free dinners, top-shelf liquor and celebrity in lieu of pay.

Debut night, he arrives with a statuesque Aussie blonde. "This is...Sabena." He lights a British Oval and passes it to her— "Darling?"—she looks like she doesn't know what hit her—then checks his Rolex and nods at me.

"Come meet the group. We'll be alternating sets." "Sets? Plural? You think we have enough material?" "Between the two of us? We could play all night."

The house band are two Malays and a Chinese, drums, keyboard and a guitar. But not just any guitar. This middle-aged Malaysian lounge musician is warming up on a *Gibson Les Paul Goldtop*. "OHMIGOD. Your guitar."

"I know." He stops playing. "It is very old," he says, sheepish, like he's apologizing for his Stradivarius.

"Old? It's a collector's..." I stop, remembering the Prime Directive. "Clapton plays one. George Harrison. So did Brian Jones!"

He chuckles. "All those pommie bastards."

"Pommies...?"

"The British. Not 'pommies.' You must never say just 'pommies.' Pommie *bastards*. Very important. Repeat!"

"Pommie *bastards*!"

"Very good. Would you like to play it?"

"Oh I couldn't.*"* I am not worthy. "But can I...hold it?"

He places the strap around my neck, and I take it gingerly in my arms.

Eventually I will work up the courage to strum a few chords on the legendary instrument all those Pommie bastards played.

Between sets visitors stream up to our table to meet us.

Their questions are mostly personal—our age, where we're from, marital status—except for one man, who says, "I am very interested to learn about your Negro slaves!"

This subject has actually never come up, what with the present-day providing so much anti-American fodder.

"Yes? What would you like to know?"

"I want know…" He lowers his voice. "How they are buy? How much they do cost?"

I wait a couple beats for him to say *just kidding*, but he doesn't. Guess I'll have to break the news.

"Abraham Lincoln freed the slaves. In 1863. Long time ago. No more slavery."

"No more slavery?" He seems crestfallen.

Spaniards has a bona fide stage, lighting and a sound system. For our intro Allan lifts the mike from the stand while I back him with a traveling blues riff.

The guy knows how to work a room. He greets VIPs, butters up the owners, leans over the stage and purrs suggestively to his date, now basking in male attention and free booze.

The audience is as diverse a crowd as I've seen since I last rode the Chicago subway: Chinese, Indians and Malaysians, Aussies, Brits, Yanks and Europeans, wealthy tourists and budget backpackers, Muslims and Hindus, Buddhists, Christians and a Jew, all of us by this time pretty well-served, so what song does Allan decide to close with, and how surprising is it that they all know *He's got the whole world in his hands?* The place goes up for grabs.

Allan improvises lyrics. He's got the Muslims and the Hindus, in his hands, He's got the Yanks and the Aussies, in his hands, He's got the Chinese and Malayans, in his hands, and on it goes, till he's got the whole room clapping and swaying and singing the gospel.

Meeting Allan removes us from our insular community and introduces us to the George Town social scene.

He says he's Thai, of royal descent, which of course

we can't verify. Although, wherever we go, people react to Allan like he's Somebody. When we're with him, doors always open and money never changes hands. He lives in Europe, speaks five languages fluently, with a knack for turning a phrase. Like this one, while we're running through some songs one afternoon. "You could be a star in Berlin."

"Uh-huh." These effusive compliments are such a part of him they hardly even sound fake.

"I'm serious." He lights an Oval. "Girl folk singers are very big there right now."

"I'm not going to Berlin."

"Because you're Jewish." He snaps his lighter shut. "It's not like that anymore. All the club owners in Berlin are Jewish." He'll introduce me, he says. We can work together. My head's in a whirl. Does this plan have any chance of success? I am a skeptic, a realist by nature. Still, his words have a certain ring: *you could be a star.*


THE FORTUNE TELLER DISAGREES.

We're in the mountains, overlooking the island—the Strait to the east, where boats and ferries bob, the rain forest and jungle to the west. Allan has arranged a day of cultural immersion for our group. We'd had a private martial arts lesson; now we're visiting a Hindu temple presided over by some palm-reading psychic.

He correctly identifies Bill as a competitive swimmer and Lin as being into handiwork. Then it's my turn.

The psychic pulls my palm in and recoils.

"THIS ONE ONLY CARES ABOUT MONEY!" He shakes his finger in my face.

"OH YEAH?"

At home I share a $175-a-month, space- heated apartment abutting the El tracks with my cousin, who's working his way through night law school. Most recently earning $155 weekly before taxes, I saved a week's salary per month and paid cash for everything. "LIKE HELL!"

Voices start stirring: a Yank is creating a scene!

"Maybe not now," the charlatan concedes. "But you will. A time will come—maybe in your fifties—when all you will think about is money. MONEY, MONEY, MONEY!" he keeps shouting at me as I walk away.

There is no mention of stardom.

We close our run at Spaniards with *Erev Shel Shoshanim*, a Buddhist and a Jew singing a Hebrew love song for a majority Muslim audience.

"This is why I travel. This is what I live for," Allan says on our last break. "The chance to make music with someone beautiful like you." His eyes are glistening with what might well be genuine emotion.

"Meet me in Bangkok, early February. I'm staying at Hotel Malaysia. We'll play some gigs, get ready for Berlin."

I tell him to go well. "*Selamat jalan,* Allan."

"*Selamat tingaal,*" he replies. "Stay well."

He hands me a little slip of paper, neatly folded and inscribed with his complete contact information and permanent address in Berlin, and I tuck it away someplace for safe keeping where it must have stayed for a very long time, because when I come across it 40 years later, I'll have no memory of ever having known his real name.

Mr. Spock says there is a theory, that "time is fluid, like a river, with currents, eddies, backwashes…"

So maybe the current that brought us Allan is the same one that swept Lin up and deposited her, that very same day, at Amat and Muna's doorstep. Hiking along a jungle path, she'd come upon a thatched-roof house and struck up conversation with the owners, a sweet older couple who'd offered to rent some rooms—the kind of deal you can only find if you speak the language.

Lin stirs sugar into her tea. "We'll get run of the place. Common room, bedroom, attic. They sleep below."

They're going to stay for a while when Mike's contract ends; I could too, till my visa expires. Also—casually spreading jam on toast—there's room for Bill.

SATURDAY NIGHT after closing Spaniards down, we tiptoe up the stairs. We listen to the cacophony of jungle night, the calls from the canopy, the close-by sound of a running stream, the distant crash of waves.

"This place," Lin whispers. "It's enchanted."

"Why are we whispering? They're not our parents."

"I know," she whispers. "So what's with your visa?"

Ah yes, my visa. I've got a house, roommates, a band, gigs; where's the rush?

On Monday I go to *Immigrasi*, fill out the forms, pay for the stamps, hand over three little pictures, all those dying vestiges of the late, great Empire, then I go home and tell Lin I extended my visa, and she says, I knew you would.

"*Dia tingaal*," she tells Amat.

He smiles, spreads his arms. "*Bagus. Saya membina rumah sendiri.*" Holds up his hands. "*Dengan dua tangan.*"

Lin asks if I'm catching any of this.

"Something about two hands?"

"Very good. *Bagus sekali.* He built this house with his own two hands."

Years ago, Amat cleared out this patch of jungle and hewed the logs to build the house. He shows us every nook and cranny. A cistern collects rain water that is piped to a spigot out back which fills a stand-up washtub. There's even a washboard. The outhouse is just steps away, convenient when refilling the bucket for the next person as etiquette demands.

The kitchen is below the house, on a concrete slab, with a wood-burning stove that Muna gathers kindling for every morning at dawn. There's a dining table and chairs, mattresses and blankets slung across homemade rattan frames. Lantern-lit, it's cozy and comfortable, somewhere they might choose to sleep on a beautiful night.

Amat points to a path behind the house that leads into the rain forest. "*Suka beranang?*"

Lin answers yes, we like to swim.

Amat waves us north. "*Jalan-jalan.*"

117

The path leads up into the mountains to a waterfall that cascades into a natural pool.

The forested hills are breathtaking, every shade of green, undulating, soft and surreal, and walking silently at the epicenter of all this life, I feel as though I'm occupying two planes—the physical here and now, and the theoretical, the ethereal—what Plato might call the Ideal.

"The sleeper has awakened."

Lin stops walking. "What did you say?"

Bill turns. "Something from Dune."

"It's like...I can see how those trees really look. In their Ideal state."

They exchange a glance, probably an eye-roll. Bill says he thinks he hears water running, and I tell them I'll catch up.

I take some pictures, but the Ideal doesn't register on film. Photos are two-dimensional, and they fade. Nothing but my memory could ever do that scene justice.

The watering hole is like from a fairy tale. Surrounded in dense foliage and rock outcroppings, a stream cascades down the rock face and spills into a natural pool. A fallen log stretches across the water.

Bill strips to his trunks, bounds up the rocks and onto the log and springs, coming up to stand in chest-deep water. He strokes all around the pond, executes a perfect underwater somersault and surfaces. "You coming in?"

Lin's in serious photog mode, she's brought her long lens and is shooting the perfect little scene from different vantage points. She shows no sign of planning to swim.

I take a picture of her taking pictures, her blonde hair gone to ringlets from the humidity.

"Let me get a shot of you on that log," she says.

I'm not crazy about this idea. "What log? I don't any log. I see a frickin' BALANCE BEAM."

"I hated those!" And we're off, cataloging everything we hated about high school. Gym! Gym teachers! Study hall! Study hall monitors! We make each other laugh till our stomachs hurt and I end up walking out onto the log. I knew I would.

Crouching with each step I end up in the exact position I'd hoped to avoid—straddling the log, with only one way off. Lin shoots a sequence with my camera, of me giggling, fighting for balance, listing further, laughing harder, until finally I've toppled, in hysterics, into the swirling waters.

On the way back, a guy up the path calls out to us: "YO! YANKS? LEMME SEE THAT FRISBEE!"

Bill is gifted at Frisbee. He arches back and throws the Frisbee far and low, curving upward to land right in the guy's hands.

"Nice catch," Bill says, when we catch up. "Whereya from?"

"Peace Corps. Joe." He's tall, a stringbean in a sarong and flour-sack shirt, with shoulder-length hair and neat beard. "I see you found the swimmin' hole. Whereya goin' now? Wanna come meet the others?"

We find Joe's contingent from the Corps seated amongst our old nemeses the Angry Aussies, back in town to raise more hell, and all of them are all singing along with the jukebox: *We don't smoke marijuana in Batu Ferringhi.*

"What the FUCK!" the best-natured Aussie bellows by way of greeting. "You arseholes still here?"

The Corps is full of esprit. They haven't left their remote villages for months, and they're party-ready.

The next record drops: *The Lion Sleeps Tonight.*

For once we Yanks have a quorum. We explode into four-part harmony with such fervor, in such a display of solidarity that the Aussies soon drop out, grumbling in their Fosters.

On the way home, it gets me thinking. "I wonder if those Aussies were right about us."

"You mean, 'the minute we meet, we're best friends?'" Lin nods. "Funny. At home we don't think of ourselves as Americans. We're Polish, Italian, Scots-Irish, whatever."

"Yeah," Bill says. "You're not really an American till you leave home.

SUNDAY MORNING AT SUNRISE Lin and I cross Muna returning from the woods with kindling. The woman performs back-breaking labor every day from dawn to dusk, always with a smile on her face, go figure, and communicates solely in high-pitched shrieks.

"*MAKAN MALAM! Masak untuk suami anda!*"

Lin blushes. "She wants to cook us all dinner tonight to celebrate my, um...husband's arrival."

"*ANDA SUKA IKAN?*" Muna squeals. "*NASI GORENG?*"

"*Ja, bagus!*" I answer. "*Suka ikan. Terimah kasih.*" She'd asked if I liked fish and fried rice, and I said I did; major communication has taken place.

"Nice," Lin says. "You actually conversed with her."

Late that afternoon on the beach, when the sun sets the tidal pools aflame, Lin spots a tall man in the tenement tee and shouts his name. She leaps to her feet and across the dunes, hurls herself into his arms and the man of her dreams—the man of just about any girl's dreams—lifts her up and twirls her around.

It's not just his looks. Mike is the whole package. Macho yet sensitive, smart and ambitious, generous and fun, he's a perfect match for Lin, the quintessential Traveling Woman.

He'd worked construction in England, hitched and bussed through Europe, Turkey and Iran, then had the *cojones* to motorcycle across Afghanistan.

"Bikin' that terrain? Kinda rough. The Afghans thought I was crazy." He shakes a few Dunhills loose for all of us. "Then I went to India and met me a purty gal. In Goa."

Among hundreds of truth-seekers and dope-doers who'd set up permanent camp on the Arabian Sea, Mike and Lin ended up at the same party the night before he was leaving.

"We're shooting the breeze, and he rests his hand on my thigh, real casual, keeps talking. I'm all, ohmigod, OHMIGOD, but he doesn't DO anything. Finally I go, 'Are you gonna kiss me OR WHAT?"

I raise my eyebrows. *Really?*

"Really," she says. "You just have no idea. Mike. Show her your passport picture."

As previously reported, 28-year-old Mike is a fine figure of a man: buff, bearded, with medium-brown hair clipped short and brushed straight back to reveal his one imperfection—a hairline receding into male-pattern baldness.

I flip the passport open. At 22, clean-shaven, with a cleft chin and full, tousled head of dishwater-blond hair, Mike was nothing short of a matinee idol. My jaw drops.

Lin laughs; just the reaction she was expecting. "Wull now, that's jist MEAN," Mike says.

Before dinner we catch them up on some of the memorable moments they've missed back home.

"Nixon's resignation." Mike fires one up. "Wish I could've seen that."

"I taped it on the Betamax at our office," I tell them. They never heard of a Betamax.

Bill reaches for the doobie. "Flew home on Air Force One the next day in tears, that fuckhead."

"They should've sent him in coach." Mike shakes his head. "And now they got this Ford asshole!"

"Actually?" Bill looks at me. "He's kind of a nice guy."

"Yeah. Like, the next-door neighbor you'd loan your snow blower.

Bill nods. "Uh-huh. Star center for Michigan. The Lions and Packers *both* went after him!"

Mike perks up. "Is that right?"

Lin cringes. "A Nixon *appointee*. That nobody elected. Is now president of the United States."

"Wull, I wouldna loaned old Tricky Dick my snow blower," Mike says. "Assumin' I had one."

"Ford's the perfect fake president for the Bicentennial," I say. "That's the big deal now. They even put out a new flag. Thirteen stars in a circle with a '76 in the middle..." and now I'm all choked up. It's this Pavlov's dog thing that always happens, like when I hear the Star-Spangled Banner at baseball games.

They look back and forth, incredulous. One president hounded out of office, the next one impeached, the Viet Nam war sputtering to an end just a few months ago, and here we are, sounding downright patriotic.

We'd gotten sick of the war, all the conflict at home, the anger. We were ready to move on, ready to let it go. So most of us had.

"They even changed the passports." Bill shows us his. It's small, navy blue, identical to the ones from the UK.

Mike reaches for it. "They're celebratin' the Bicentennial by givin' us *British* passports? Idden that ironic?" It looks tiny in his hands. "Well...least now they can't sort ours out'n send us to the back of the line at customs. Don'tcha hate that?" He takes out his, the old over-sized olive drab like Lin's and mine. "Even so, I'd as soon hang onto this one. Jist added some more pages. Again."

"Me too," Lin says.

Bill and I straighten up. "You guys hadda ADD PAGES?" We're in the presence of greatness.

Amat leads us below, to a lantern-lit dining table set for four. *"Saya dibina yang."*

"He built the table," Lin says.

I crack my first joke in Bahasa. *"Denga dua tengan?"*

Muna cackles. It's his pet phrase. Amat does everything with his own two hands.

He goes in search of something he might have to fix while Muna ladles out mounds of *nasi goreng* topped with chunks of steaming fish poached in a fiery sauce. She then remains, looming over us—to the extent someone 4' 9" can be said to loom—shaking her hands and squealing MAKAN! MAKAN! throughout the meal, like any Yiddische *bubbe* shouting ES! ES! at her grandchildren.

Funny, when I first started traveling, all I noticed was how different everything seemed. Now I'm so much more struck by the similarities.

After dinner Bill and I bus up to Telok Bahang. It's the next town up the road and there's not much to it—a small grocery, a café, and between them, where you'd expect to find a barber shop, or a hardware store, in a concrete building with no windows and a picnic bench out front, is the opium den.

Bill spots it from the bus. "There. HOLY SHIT. Is that...?" He bounds down the stairs. "My old travel partner. EDDIE!"

Eddie is Bill's age, cute, with shortish brown hair and the requisite mustache. He's in Penang on two missions.

The first is to witness the Hindu festival of Thaipusam, which has been banned in India because it's too barbaric—*too barbaric for INDIA?*—and the second is to visit this opium den. "So? You guys ready?"

Bill looks at me. *You coming?*

I get up and follow them in. I knew I would.

The opium den is like a scene out of one of those herky-jerky old newsreels with the dramatic voiceover: *The Scourge of Addiction!* A few red bare bulbs screwed into the wall, patrons lying prone on long stone slabs with their eyes closed, men shuffling back and forth lighting people's pipes.

A Chinese guy checks us in like for a dental appointment: lie back, relax; no food or drink for a while after.

A tiny, wizened man with cloudy eyes escorts me to my slab. He motions I should lean back, rolls a stone pillow beneath my head, sits cross-legged beside me, puffs on the long-stemmed stone pipe, gets it gurgling like a dirty bong, then proceeds to totally bogart till I take it out of his hands.

The smoke is mild, though I don't care for the medicinal flavor. I take a few hits and lie back on the stone pillow, waiting to feel something. "How long's it supposed to take?"

The little man smiles, finishes off my allotment and collapses, coughing. His chest gurgles just like the pipe.

On the way out I pass Bill and Eddie, eyes still closed, prone on their stones.

Waiting outside, I'm jittery and on edge. What's taking them so long? Now I'm queasy. And people get addicted to these sensations? This is horrible. I buy a soda next door and sip it at the picnic table, waiting for the carbonation to settle my stomach. It doesn't.

Nausea rises from my gut, to my chest, to my throat, until that feeling of inevitability overcomes me and I lurch to the street, drop to my knees and heave up the best meal I ever ate on the Overland Trail.

Around the time everything stops spinning, Bill finds me propped up against a tree, "Jesus! Whatsamatter!"

"I threw up."

Eddie comes up behind him.

"She threw up!" Bill looks alarmed, concerned, very sweet.

"Really?" Eddie has a dreamy expression. "I don't feel nauseous at all."

"Me either," Bill says. "I feel this...clarity. I'm not even drowsy. I thought I would be." He looks at me. "So you feel absolutely nothing?"

I concentrate. "Anxious. My heart's racing."

"Gee, that sucks," Eddie says.

"It gave me an upset stomach, so I got a lemonade next door..."

"Rookie mistake," a Yank voice says.

Two Americans at the picnic table are waiting to go in. "You can't drink anything right after," the girl says.

This sort of rings a bell. "Oh. Yeah. Dammit."

"Couple more times," the guy says, like a spotter in the gym encouraging me to do a few more reps. "You build up a tolerance."

I remember John in Bali, heaving Magic Mushroom pizza in a ditch. *When the body says no...* "Never again."

"We're goin' in," the guy says. "You gonna hang for a while?"

"Wait up," says Eddie. "Bill? 'Nother round?"

He looks at me. "I'll stay here."

They emerge with faces glowing. "Great to be back,"

the guy says. They're English teachers in Japan, making good money. At the end of each semester they come here, dope up for a few weeks, then go back to work in Japan. They've been at this a couple years now, teaching English and smoking opium.

"What about withdrawal?"

"A couple bad days," the girl says. "No big deal."

We hang around longer than I'd have devoted to these two, but Bill isn't budging so we miss the last bus and leave Eddie sprawled out on the picnic table, as he's not up to a three-mile walk just then, even though it's all downhill, and the night is beautiful.

At a bend in the road, the Strait comes into view, illuminated by moon glow, pointing our way east.

The jungle has fallen silent. We hear only crickets, the surf, our own footsteps.

"I feel like I could walk all night," Bill says.

I stumble on some loose gravel and he takes my hand. "Careful, city girl. Pick up your feet! Like this." He tramps ahead. "See? This is how you walk in the country."

Hand in hand we stroll in the moonlight. "Should I come with you to Thailand?" His tone is very sweet.

"Yes. You should."

He guides me through the darkness to our porch, where we sit and listen to the night song.

"We should sleep together tonight," he whispers.

"We should."

"I mean, just sleep. Not make love."

"I know," I whisper. "That's what I meant." Still, I'm struck by his word choice. Not have sex, or get it on: make love. He is a sweet man.

We stretch out on Amat and Muna's double bed and talk till the roosters crow. Bill's broken engagement, the subsequent live-in girlfriend who'd hung him out to dry; my first love, the keyboard player, my next love, his best friend, who played lead guitar—the one I'd married.

He hadn't gone home like I did when the beatings started at the convention in '68; he'd been clubbed and arrested and thrown in a paddy wagon.

"Best friends," Bill says. "Talk about a cliché."

"I know, right? We were stupid. Too young. I'd just turned 20. It lasted senior year of college. One day our new lease comes in the mail. He goes, I don't want to renew this. I go, me either. That was that. A lot of the wedding presents still had tags on them."

"Fancy wedding?"

"Nah. It was 1971. I got my wedding dress at a basement sale."

Bill props himself up on an elbow. "So it was mutual. Neither of you got hurt."

I watch the fan blades twirl. "Yeah. Mutual." *We both did.* "I remember when I called my gramma to tell her we were splitting up. She said, 'I'm sorry you feel sad, but...he wasn't for you. You need a man who fights back.' And he didn't. He fought the police, he fought for his convictions... but when we started drifting apart—that he didn't fight."

"Hmm. You seeing anyone now?"

"Kinda," I say. "Nothing serious."

"Me too," he says. "Me either."

The next morning I wake to a telltale poke. We've drifted together in our sleep, and Bill is in the early-morning manly way. I sense from his breathing that he's awake, that he knows I know he is awake, and is waiting to see how I will react. It's our moment of truth: turn to him or roll away?

I roll and make a little sleep-sigh so we can both pretend this never happened. Later I'll get the impression he didn't much care, he just finally wanted to know one way or the other.

Around the time Muna's firing up the cookstove I find Lin at the spigot out back.

"Get in late?" she asks.

"Crazy night." I fill her in: the opium den, Eddie,

the hurled dinner, the Yank junkies, the missed bus, the moonlit stroll. "Uh-huh." She's through playing guessing games. "So. Are you and Bill...?"

"No." This can now be answered definitively.

"Oh." She looks disappointed. "We were—well, Mike was like, 'do you think they are?' and I was like, 'I dunno,' and he says, 'Wull I hope so, so they're not hearin' us.'" She seems genuinely embarrassed.

"I didn't hear a thing."

"Are you...*really*? We got kinda loud last night...."

"Really." So *this* is why she'd insisted on the attic. Amat and Muna slept directly below the bedroom Bill and I now shared. "Unless I mistook you for some orang utans..."

"Very funny." She gives me a shove, and then, from the house, we hear Amat screaming.

*"MUNA! MUNA! RAZAK MATI!"*

"*Mati*," Lin says. "Somebody died."

When we reach him, our smiling, happy surrogate grandpa is wailing. "*Perdana Menteri Razak! MATI!*"

Mike comes outside. "What's goin' on?"

"Somebody died," Lin says. "Razak?"

Mike lays a steady hand on Amat's shoulder. "Abdul Razak Hussein. The prime minister. Awww. He wudden a well man. That's jist a shame."

"*Saya maaf*, Amat." Lin says she's sorry.

"*Bagus orang?*" I ask. Good man?

"*Bagus orang.*" Amat nods.

"Yes he was," Mike says. "'Specially for these here folks. Built schools, spread the wealth around, quieted down all that ruckus between the Malays and Chinese..."

"*Begitu muda*," Muna croaks. "*Awal lima puluh.*"

"Young man. Early fifties." Lin translates.

All day from loudspeakers and radios comes the chanting of *muezzins* that sounds so Hebraic to me.

Amat listens to the prayers and speeches, performing his daily chores and looking hopelessly sad.

A couple days later, I find Bill scowling in the bedroom, his arms folded.

"We gotta talk. About this." He points to my valise. "I don't travel with people who carry that kind of bag."

I chuckle.

"Oh, I'm serious. 'You hardly have anything to carry. Can you take this for me?'" he says in that snotty high-pitched voice men use to mimic women. "Never fails. I travel light, 'cause I don't wanna carry shit, then other people try to get me to carry their shit."

He makes me empty everything on the bed and sort it into two piles: stuff I'm taking, and stuff I'm sending home. "I'm gonna give you a lesson in packing."

I decide to play along and start sorting as he debates my decisions. "A turtleneck sweater? In the tropics?"

"It'll be cold in Europe."

He lets my plaid flannel shirt pass, watching silently with lips pursed. "Too many tee-shirts. You just need two. What the hell is this?" He picks up the purple tie-dye outfit.

"It's nice and lightweight." I don't like him handling my clothes.

"I've never seen you in it. SHIP!"

Home go the flour-sack outfits, some pants and long-sleeved shirts. "You've read those books. Get rid of 'em."

"I need them to trade."

He seizes upon my towel. "Way too thick and bulky. Get one like mine."

His towel is thin, scratchy, institutional-issue; hardly bigger than a hand-towel. Mine is a plush, harvest-gold, double-loop terry-cloth bath sheet, occasionally used as a blanket. I snatch it from him. "The towel stays."

Now he's going through my Ziploc bag of toiletries. "Clairol Herbal Essence shampoo *and* conditioner. Ridiculous. Two unnecessary items. Just use soap."

"On my HAIR?"

He capitulates. "Awright. I think this'll work. Gimme that batik you carry around like your little security blanket."

I pass him my second-hand blue batik. I've not seen Bill's bossy side previously and am not too crazy about it.

"Now *pay attention.*" He secures the batik, towel and hanging items in the outer flap, then rolls and tucks the other clothes along the edge of the pack, creating a well in the center for the hard goods: toiletries, sandals, books, my radio and clock. Everything fits.

"Holy crap. Everything fits."

Bill spreads his hands. "My work is done."

Now would be a logical time to discuss where we're going next, but a new Stones album is blasting from the attic. We race to the garret, tucked in the eaves of the house.

Mike opens the door, shirtless, crouching. "Come on in."

It's breezy up here, not the oven I was expecting, with screened windows and a rotating fan. Their gear is neatly stacked on a broom swept plank floor—sleeping bags, a fancy tape player and heap of cassettes.

"Whadda y'all wanna hear?"

"STICKY FINGERS!" Bill takes a hit from the pipe Lin passes him and starts playing air bass-guitar, his mood vastly improved.

I pick up a cassette. "Imagine if you could hook a pair of headphones up to a little tiny tape player. Wouldn't that be cool?" I'm going to be pretty mad at Sony for stealing my idea when the Walkman comes out.

"Sure would!" Mike thinks for a moment. "Problem is, the tape. All that windin' 'n rewindin' to get to the song you wanna hear. Very inefficient. A disk makes more sense. But you got that damn needle. Still. There's oughta be a way..."

"Don't get him going," Lin says. "You know how many sentences he starts with 'There oughta be a way?'"

"Cassettes suck." Bill says. "I like albums. I like album covers. They're works of art." He holds up the cassette. "On the album cover, this," he points to Jagger's crotch, "is an actual zipper. And howya supposed to roll a joint on this?"

We all laugh, but one day, cassettes and CDs will both be passe, while the vinyl record spins on.

At HIGH NOON the day of the full moon, Bill. Eddie and I line up in to observe the Hindu faithful celebrate Thaipusam.

Eddie says the festival commemorates a deity vanquishing some demon.

"They started out last night, downtown, at moonrise, following a silver-painted chariot carrying a statue of this… Lord Somebody…"

"Lord Muruga," a British voice says. We all turn.

"Lord Muruga defeated a foe using a holy spear given him by the Lord Shiva," says a man in a bush hat.

"TREVOR!"

"As ever. Pardon the interruption," Trevor says. "Go on."

"They smash coconuts all over the street," Eddie says.

"Signifying the shattering of one's own ego, so I've read." Trevor nods to Eddie.

"Everybody gives offerings. Fruit, flowers, incense, milk. Lotta milk. They bring their babies to be blessed."

"By the statue." *Thou shalt have no craven images before me,* my Hebrew God thunders. "Uh-huh."

"It's *symbolic*," Eddie says. "Then the penitents—they fast for two days—carry these…uh…"

"*Kavadis.*" Trevor's on tiptoe, peering through the crush of onlookers. "Burdens. Earthen pots of milk, balanced on their heads, or suspended from a long staff across their shoulders. Or they pull chariots. Then come the *vel kavadis*— portable altars, which are…" he clears his throat—"affixed to the bearers. As you'll soon see. There she is. I should put a tether on that woman. Well then. Take care, Yankee bird."

"So long, Trevor."

He weaves through the crowd to Trish, who's chatting up a group of barefoot Hindu women in brilliantly colored orange and yellow saris, all waving peacock feathers.

Lord Muruga arrives on the silver chariot.

The drums thunder, the music is deafening, the heat ferocious; incense wafting, riots of color, a total assault on the senses.

The chariot begins its ascent to the hilltop temple, followed by bare-footed men in loincloths carrying milk pots.

Then the young men carrying the *kavadis* can proceed.

A teenage boy comes first. A long metal spear is inserted through his cheeks, forcing his mouth open; a foot-long spike pierces his tongue. As he passes a woman darts from the crowd, crowing with pride as she pours a bottle of orange pop over his tongue. He doesn't notice her, or the orange pop. The skin surrounding the spear is whitish- grey. There's no sign of blood.

Another man is pulling an ornate wheeled cart. But not with his hands. It is roped to six or so massive, heavy meat hooks buried in his back. As he bends to drag the cart uphill, an older man pulls it in the opposite direction, stretching his skin. He's in no apparent pain.

Dozens more men pass us, impaled by spikes and spears, in no apparent distress, staring fixedly ahead to the steps leading to the temple.

Finally come the *vel kavadi* carriers, beneath small altars from which long metal spikes protrude. Inserted deep into their chests and backs, these spikes bear the weight of the altar. Some of the bearers also have spikes through their tongues, or spears through their cheeks.

As the most devout, or penitent, the *vel kavadi* carriers are what Westerners might call the honor guard, aware enough of their surroundings to stop to be photographed or receive devotions from the onlookers.

All this time, the drumming and music blast ceaselessly, deafeningly, in hundred-degree heat.

We follow the procession to the steps of Waterfall Temple. Everyone is permitted to climb 512 stairs to watch the spears, spikes and hooks being bloodlessly, painlessly removed, then join with the faithful, whirling in ecstasy until nightfall.

We decide not to stay for that part.

Bill doesn't get up when the bus stops at Mama's. "I'm staying in Telok Bahang tonight, with Eddie. You could maybe work on your photo albums."

While you smoke opium? "Aye, Captain."

He smiles, but I see he's gotten the point.

Lin and Mike are out when I get home. "VROOM VROOM," Amat says, pantomiming shifting gears.

"They rented a motorcycle?"

He nods, moves his finger in a circle. *"Pergi di sekitar pulau, makan malam George Town."*

"They're driving around the island and having dinner in George Town?

*"Ja."* He changes the subject. *"Berapa Thaipusam?"*

Charades. I clap my hand over my heart, widen my eyes, then poke my fingers deep into my cheek. I gesture high above my head, and stoop down, like someone carrying something tall and heavy. I splay my fingers across my chest, showing him the spikes. I pound drums, cover my ears, wincing, and end with a shrug, palms up, as if to ask, what does it mean?

"Hindus." He points to imaginary beings standing before us, showing they worship many gods. "Allah. Allah. Allah. Allah." Then he turns to me, hand over his heart.

*"Amat percaya satu Allah."* One God. He raises one finger and points to heaven. *"ALLAH!"*

One God, the same God. The same word in Hebrew and Arabic, just pronounced a little differently. So what is it we're fighting about, exactly? Religion? Or real estate?

Bill returns from Telok Bahang the next day all smiles and jokes. He launders his icky towel and few pairs of underwear and tee-shirts in my Rinso and hangs them on the line. "Awright, city girl. Where we goin' next?"

We pore over The Book, study my tiny Atlas, consult with Mike and Lin.

"Meet us in Bangkok," she says. "We're booked at the Federal starting the 3rd."

"Stay outta the Eastern provinces," Mike says. "Too close to Laos."

"Really? Vientiane sounds so cool in The Book."

"It was," Lin says. "They called it the Paris of the East. Canals, boulevards…"

"Bombed all to hell," Mike says. "State's just issued a travel alert. That right-wing government we were proppin' up got ousted last month. Ho's runnin' the show."

Bill gives me a look. "We're not going to Laos. What's Phuket like?"

"Gorgeous. Great divin' and snorkelin'—touristy though. Lotta Thai girls plyin' the trade…"

This is not a ringing endorsement. "We'll see," Bill says.

AMAT JOINS US on the porch while we smoke up the weed we don't dare carry across the border. Bill passes him the pipe. The old man shakes his head no, then reaches for it.

"*Jangan beritahu Muna.*"

Lin laughs. She promises we won't tell Muna and I pose them for a picture, against a backdrop of sarongs fluttering from the thatched roof.

Mike's in a rattan chair, legs crossed, shirtless and deeply tanned, in boot-cut levis.

The others are around the banquette Amat built with his own two hands. Bill is also dark, bearded and bare-chested in the heat. Lin's in cutoffs and a tank top, flashing those dimples, and smiling beside her is 60-year-old Amat. White-haired, nearly toothless, in a sleeveless white undershirt and sarong knotted around his waist, he looks ancient.

But one day I'll look at this picture and see Amat as lean and strong, happy and healthy, a much more vital man than I remembered, when I am older than he was then.

# chicago
January 11, 2016

## *T*HE SLEEPER AWAKENS

I crossed the equator that Christmas Eve in 1975 as someone who'd been looking through a kaleidoscope, watching colors combine in random beautiful patterns and sitting back to enjoy the view.

On the Java Sea I hit some turbulence. I exchanged the kaleidoscope for a spyglass, a charmingly antiquated instrument, appropriate for the colonial sites I'd visit, yet capable of zooming in, of gaining perspective.

Observing those weeks along the Strait through today's digital lens, it appears that's what happened. I focused: my perceptions went from general to specific, hazy to distinct; the sleeper had awakened.

I'd stopped viewing the natives as an aggregate— *Easterners*, *Asians*—started discerning their ethnic and cultural distinctions. People I'd originally seen as men in skirts all shouting in my face were becoming friends and surrogate family I could relate to as peers.

Still later, I'd see them as noble, admirable, heroic. Through their eyes I'd see the role colonization played in shaping these places and people, the wedge it drove between not only East and West, but among them.

An analysis of how various colonizers affected the long-term development of these countries is best put forth by scholars and historians. What I saw up close was how centuries of subservience damaged individuals, how it put them on guard, forced them to jockey for position amongst each other, to internalize the notion that East is least and West is best, how it affected their very posture and ability to make eye contact with white people.

Thailand would drive these perceptions home. The Thai had capitalized on the West, done business with the *farang.* The would-be colonizers would not succeed in subjugating Siam. They liked Americans; they'd had dealings with us. They'd thrived under U.S. protection, and profited by it.

So among them I felt the most at home, accepting and accepted, comfortable in my Western skin, sensing less of a barrier between *us* and *them.*

Aside from these global issues there were some personal ones, of mostly the classic coming-of-age variety. Would I have the guts to leave my conventional life behind, the talent and drive to make it as a musician? Find true love? Pursue a career? It was time to decide.

It helped that I'd made friends I could really talk to, who truly got me, who traveled with me for the rest of the journey. I opened up about the marital experiment that went bust, some dubious choices I'd made.

I talked about my grandmother—the "astral twin" whose birthday I shared and whose presence I so often sensed, and especially, I faced head on the death of my father in early childhood.

Long dormant memories of him surfaced on page after page of my journal.

Removed from my parents and with contact between us suspended, free of their pressure to pack up those sorrows and always make nice, I was finally free to think about, and grieve for, the gifted man of such varied interests and talents who had been taken so young, and taken from me when I was so young.

What started as a quest for my identity became a lesson in how others saw me. White. A woman. A Yank. Very broad categories, just like I put them in. But I was different in one respect. And I was truly experiencing it for the first time.

I'd grown up surrounded by people just like me. I'd never felt like one of a minority. Then I got to Asia.

In the months and miles I traveled between Hong Kong and Jerusalem, I can count the number of other Jews I met on one hand. Chancing upon each other in remote settings, the link was instantaneous, telepathic. Kind of like we were all logged on to the same network: members of a tribe, *Landsmenn,* wherever we were, always together, always The Others.

And that otherness was our badge of honor, our special connection to the tribal people we encountered whose traditions were also vanishing and numbers dwindling.

During this time I acquired one new identity—as an Overlander.

We were a migratory people, with hierarchy and status, a social structure, barter system, and interesting gender dynamics that were the subject of many stoned raps.

Perceived in traditional roles by the people surrounding us, we found ourselves drifting back into them: women doing laundry by hand, men hauling backpacks onto the *bemos* and keeping the curious throngs of local men at bay. We traveling women were so few in number, so vulnerable, brazen, in denial—especially the handful of us who chose to go it alone—but all along the Trail, our traveling brothers closed ranks around us. They were deferential, protective; it was comfortable, familiar; reminiscent of our idyllic 1950s childhoods, when Moms wore shirtwaists and Fathers knew best. But it was temporary.

We would return to our enlightened, conflicted homelands and our modern, complicated relationships, and never again would I have such a positive outlook on men.

We created a community without borders to become citizens of the world; we renounced labels, the class system and rigid structure of the hated Establishment, then we turned right around and instituted our own.

You were a traveler, or a tourist, you were cool, or an asshole. Political correctness was years off. Sweeping generalizations about the different nationalities were formed and readily accepted. A certain pecking order emerged.

The Brits had top status. That was natural. We were on their former turf, there was the familial connection, the feeling of shared DNA. And giving credit where due, I found the British were typically the best-informed about the places and cultures we visited; thoughtful and mindful, as though they retained some sense of responsibility towards them.

The Germans dominated among the Western Europeans. They were the largest contingent, the canniest travelers, the most frugal, able to withstand the greatest hardship and the least sanitation. Sleeping among bedbugs or on chairs didn't daunt them; they were tough.

The Dutch were industrious, well-liked, well-connected; the Scandinavians enlightened and evolved; New Zealanders fun-loving and friendly, with entirely different dispositions from their brothers Down Under.

Given their global reputation for friendliness it's surprising how many people the Aussies alienated. But no one did they honk off more than the North Americans.

In Southeast Asia Canadians and Yanks were a solid front, united against them, but in Europe that alliance broke down. As our census grew, the balance tilted. The Canadians divorced us. They took pains to distinguish themselves from us. They sewed maple leaves on their backpacks, and who could blame them?

In Europe the Americans were the assholes, and the Aussies were awesome, and it was there that one of life's great lessons began to dawn on me—that the ultimate measure of cool is not where you're from, but how far you've come.

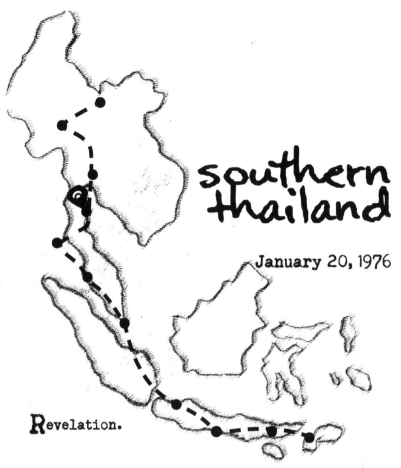

# southern thailand

**January 20, 1976**

Revelation.

We bungle getting out of Malaysia.

We miss the dawn bus out of Batu Ferringhi, so we miss the first ferry to the mainland and get to the Butterworth station just as the northbound bus to the border is pulling away.

"Shit," says Nebraska Bill who is really from Queens. "What time is it?" Neither of us wears a watch.

The next bus leaves in 4 hours.

"Four hours!" We're scouting for some shade. Bill's pissed. "I'm surprised at you. I thought you were the type to get us to the bus on time."

So now I'm pissed. How's this my fault? It's not like we have somewhere to be. We don't even know where we're going.

139

I lean against a tree and open the Graham Greene novel I've been saving.

"Gimme that Yellow Book." Bill flips through *Southeast Asia on a Shoestring,* scowling, then tosses it on the ground. He jiggles his feet, drums his fingers, crosses and uncrosses his arms. Finally, he puts on his straw fedora with a snarky *watch my stuff* and strides off to wander around Butterworth, which, according to The Book, lacks George Town's charm.

Hours later, a trishaw driver pedals up pulling Bill. "Finally! Jesus Christ! Where've you been? I have to pee. Do you remember if there's a WC in the train station?"

"I dunno." This will be Bill's stock answer to any question I pose; he's put me in charge of noticing things. He reaches for my pack. "Are we out of cigarettes?"

"Where were you all that time?"

"Just—around. I had to get rid of some...uh...opium."

"WHAT!" This border is infamous. Overlanders kept waiting for hours, getting searched and hassled and jailed and deported, and he was going to cross carrying opium?

"I SAID I got rid of it!"

"You smoked OPIUM in PUBLIC?"

"NO! I tipped my driver with it."

During the entire jangling three-hour bus ride, through hilly forest and jungle, swaying palms and banana trees, passing rubber plantations and terraced farms, I exclaim over the scenery while Bill keeps his fedora plastered over his face.

We reach the border around 4 o'clock. There's no line. A customs officer stamps our passports without even glancing at our bags and points us towards a wide-open, creepy No Man's Land that stretches to the Thai checkpoint.

"We could've had a kilo on us," Bill grouses.

"Uh-huh. Or we could've been strip searched." I slip on my backpack, prop my guitar over my shoulder and, excess baggage finally shed, slog beside Bill across the muddy, marshy ground into Thailand.

"Awright!" he says on the other side, like he's about to take charge. "What town are we going to?"

"Had Yai." For the fourth time.

Some Aussies coming south tell us the bus to Had Yai is a beast: three hours over bad roads.

"Crap," I say. "Happen to know where I can change a traveler's check?"

"At the bank in Had Yai."

Bill flips out. "WHAT! You don't have any CASH?"

"The taxi drivers'll take your Yank money." The Aussies walk away, snickering.

"THREE HOURS!" Bill says. "Fuck that. TAXI!"

We approach a Thai guy leaning against a '59 Chevy Bel Air. "How much to Had Yai?"

"Thirty US dollah."

Bill reaches for his wallet.

"No way," I say. "Ten!"

"Twenty-fi!" the driver cries.

"We're getting outta here." Bill's tone is ominous. He hasn't shown signs of a temper before, but we've advanced 75 miles in 10 hours. We're hot and thirsty, hungry and tired, and it's all my fault.

"We're not paying $12.50 apiece—three days budget—for a taxi ride."

"WE?" he hisses. "You're not paying anything. NO CASH! What were you THINKING?"

What was *I* thinking, opium boy? "Just gimme a minute. Got a nice, clean ten?" Crisp cash gets to them; in this climate their money always wilts.

He hands me one.

Circling thumb and forefinger under my tongue I blast an ear-splitting whistle. Everyone nearby snaps to attention, including Bill. "Holy crap! I never saw a chick do that."

"HAD YAI!" I scream, waving the greenback aloft. "TEN US DOLLAH!"

"OKAY OKAY!" says Bel Air guy. "I take you Had Yai." As we clamber into the back seat, Bill stifles a smile.

I look around the Chevy. "I think we had this car when I was little."

"Everyone did," Bill says. "Got a match?"

"I got match," the driver says. "You got cigarette?"

Bill looks at me. "Welcome to Thailand, city girl."

We speed north through villages that remind me of the old-time Wild West. Just as I'd sensed the ghost of Britain in Malaysia, I feel an American presence here, in the wide gravel roads and plank sidewalks, the clusters of one-story wooden storefronts.

"It's like something out of a cowboy movie. Except for the palm trees."

Bill grunts, and closes his eyes, not even looking out the window after everything he's gone through to get here.

Had Yai caters to GIs and Malaysian tourists. It's full of gambling and girls, restaurants and cheap rooms.

"I'll go find the bank," I tell Mr. Sunshine.

"Forget it. I'm starving. Let's just get situated."

We pick the Hotel Mandarin: private bath, double bed, Western toilets, air conditioning: 100 baht.

"Twenty baht to the dollar. So easy to calculate!"

Bill peels off a five and shoves the register at me.

On our way into a café we pass some Germans leaving—a tall, nice-looking man with two short drunks: Frank's boys.

The tall one nods at me. *"Guten abend. Können wir sprechen?"*

*"Ja, sicher. Wie gehts? Wo ist Frank?"* Yes, where *is* cute, fun, kiss-on-the-cheek Frank?

The little guys nudge each other and giggle.

"Be right there," I tell Bill. When he's out of earshot I say, "OK, what's the deal?"

"Frank went home. He became...ill."

"Dysentery?"

"No. He caught a...disease." He pauses to let me figure out what *kind* of disease. "Before he met you. He was very concerned about you."

142

Okay, this explained a lot. "He shouldn't have been. There was nothing between us."

"He said you shared a...cigarette." He pauses to show he knows what *kind* of cigarette. "You should have yourself checked." And he motions to his boys to follow.

Six months after we parted in Jogja, I'll get a sweet, apologetic letter from Frank. He'd been misdiagnosed; false alarm.

I find Bill chugging a Singha. "Who were those guys?"

"Some Germans I met in Jogja." Fortunately, there's no reason to share the substance of the conversation with Bill. "How's the beer?"

"Not bad. Pretty good." He doesn't speak again. Back in the room, he says, "Goin' out."

Good. Don't let the door hitya in the ass.

Hours later, I awaken to the sound of him whizzing with the bathroom door open. A teenage boy is standing beside the bed.

"WHAT the FUCK!" I pull the covers up to my neck.

"This is my friend." The toilet flushes. "I got us a Thai stick. Where's the papers?"

He knows damn well I hide the EZ Widers in my box of tampons, where customs officials are unlikely to search.

"I'm not dressed. Get 'em yourself."

Bill twists one up and moistens the entire thing in his mouth just like I hate, then turns the air-conditioning on full blast. "Where's the lighter?"

We pass the joint in the near-dark, listening to a crackling broadcast from Armed Forces radio. The boy starts wheezing and sniffling.

"Your friend is freezing." I pull the covers tightly around my shoulders. No one says anything else.

When Bill carefully stubs out the roach the kid leaps to his feet, intones, *"Sawa dī,"* ducks his head politely and bolts.

*"Lā kon ka,"* I answer. The door closes.

With this language I'm going to have my work cut out. Not only do males and females use different word endings, it's tonal. Words change meaning according to the pitch at which they're spoken. The result is a bunch of disjointed, sing-song syllables you can hardly mimic, let alone decipher.

Bill sits in the chair with his arms crossed. Finally he moderates the air-conditioning, takes off his jeans and climbs in, him hugging the edge, me plastered against the wall, like a long-married couple going to bed mad.

He's fake-sleeping the next morning when I slip out to a sidewalk cafe to consider my options over a cup of alarmingly orange Ceylon tea. *Bill's an asshole. I'll just go to Bangkok myself. Am I ready for that?* Tastes okay, just looks weird. *Phuket, maybe? Nah, too touristy.* Gotta find a bank.

And now here he comes, my travel companion, showered and smelling agreeably of Clairol Herbal Essence.

We each wait for the other to say something. "How was the shower?"

"Cold." He sits down, tips the chair back, crosses and uncrosses his arms.

"I'll go find a bank."

"Yeah. Look, uh...we gotta talk." We finally make eye contact. Bill clears his throat. "I was thinkin'...about. Goin' on by myself."

I stare down, stir the tea, letting his words hang out there, then look up at him, lips twitching.

"What?"

"I was just gonna tell you...that I was thinking about... going on by myself. Same exact words."

He smiles, looking relieved. A tiny three-wheeled open cab flits past us, emitting visibly noxious fumes.

Bill coughs. Something scurries amongst the cigarette butts, fruit peels and newspapers in the gutter. "Awright. So. Finish that...orange stuff. We gotta get out of this place."

"If it's the last thing we ever do." And just like that, we're speaking to each other in song lyrics, friends again.

I shower under a chilly drip while Bill rolls a couple doobies for the road and pores over The Book the way one might stand at an open refrigerator, waiting for something new to appear.

Had Yai is the travel hub of Southern Thailand, where all roads and rail lines converge. We're on a narrow strip of land between the Gulf of Siam to the east and the Andaman Sea—part of the Indian Ocean—on the West.

"You can get anywhere on the isthmus from here," I call from the bathroom. "Was there just the one towel?" He got to it first. Ick. "Isthmus—isthmus. That's really hard to say."

"So stop saying it. C'mon. You ready to check out of the Ritz?" The room doesn't look so hot in daylight. We've had it with Had Yai.

We find a bank and I try to settle up but he waves me off. "Keep it. Where's the train station? I'm not getting on another bus."

We look around helplessly at signs we can't read as traffic whirls around us: motorbikes, Yank tanks, pedicabs, push bikes and three-wheeled tuk-tuks, darting out of nowhere, coming up on the sidewalk, changing directions and crossing lanes at whim.

"Ohmigod, these people drive like maniacs."

"Welcome to Thailand, city girl."

The train to Phuket leaves at noon and takes nine hours, whereas a train for someplace called Surat Thani is leaving shortly and takes only takes six.

"Forget Phuket." Bill nods at me. "Pay the man."

At a sidewalk market, we buy some fruit for the train. "Pay up."

So *this* is the deal. He's going to teach me a lesson, make me reach for my wallet every few feet, force me to keep track of everything.

"This fruit isn't going to get us through the day," he says. "What else is there? Let's get some of that pop."

I pay a lady two baht for a neon-hued soda while her kids jump and point at us. *Farang! Farang!* Allan has told me this means 'round-eyes,' but it's not used in a pejorative sense, merely descriptive.

"These words are all related. Isn't that interesting? *Farang, ferringhi,* foreign." No response. "Here. It's all yours."

He takes a big gulp and grimaces.

"I know, right? The first sip is always the worst."

Bill spends most of the train ride with his hat over his face. Getting there isn't half the fun for him, it's no fun at all, whereas my trip starts the minute I leave the house. Why these contrary types so often end up traveling together, and marrying each other, is something I'll ponder in the future.

Hours later we detrain beside a muddy river after what I describe to Bill as a not terribly scenic ride up isthmus.

"Still beat the hell out of a bus ride, jouncing from pothole to pothole. Plus there was a bathroom."

"Oh. Yeah." Squatting on a rocking train over a hole in the floor that drains onto the tracks, privates in the breeze; I suppose you could call it that. "Hey." I elbow him. "Isn't that Peace Corps Joe?"

Towering above the crowd, with shoulder-length hair, in gold wire-rims and a flour-sack shirt, the man turns.

"That's him. HEY PEACE CORPS!"

The man beside him turns around.

Joe's buddy is Eric. Also with the Corps, he's an inch or so shorter than lanky Joe, broad-shouldered, with close-cropped, wavy blond hair, a handlebar mustache, and Clark Kent-style tortoise shell horn-rims.

"Nebraska! Chicago! Whereya goin'?" They're headed to Koh Samui, an island in the Gulf.

"It's not built up, no one's really goin' there yet. You get there on an all-night ferry."

We look at each other. No one's goin' there yet? We'll be able to say *we* got someplace first?

"We're in," Bill says. We've both figured out we get along better as part of a group.

The crowds part to let us pass. Nobody shouts, tries to sell us stuff, gets up in our faces. Kids who jump and point are shooshed. People wave, or flash peace signs, and smile. *Americans*, some of them murmur. The word sounds like music. *Americans*. They like us here.

The fare on the all-night ferry is 20 baht—one dollar—to spend the night on wooden benches below deck. An extra 10 baht gets us sleep mats on deck. The operator shows us some rolled-up foam camping mattresses.

Joe snaps his fingers. "We'll take 'em!"

Bill nods. "Pay the man."

We eat sticky rice and satay from a street stall, have some beers, wander aimlessly around the dock.

"Hours yet." Joe strokes his beard, then resolutely flicks his cigarette into a garbage-choked ditch.

"Hey," Bill says. "Ya dropped something." He's a trash vigilante, far ahead of his time.

"Creates jobs for people, picking up all this crap. You two"—to me and Eric—"watch our stuff." He taps Bill's shoulder. "You're with me."

Long after dark they return, mission accomplished. "Lookit *this*." Bill crouches beside me and unwraps a foil packet that contains a big chunk of dark, sticky, aromatic hashish. "Koh Samui is gonna rock."

Around 11 o'clock we bound up to the deck with our foam pads while a group of Germans troops down to cargo.

"Yanks. *Schwächlinge*," one mutters.

Weaklings? Oh yeah? I smile at them, snarky-sweet. *"Schlaf gut auf deinen Stühlen."*

AT DAWN WE DOCK in Na Thon, the island's only town. The Germans immediately separate from us. All but one—a skinny, bushy-bearded guy with a fright-wig head of brown hair stands frozen between our two groups.

"ANDY!" The head German shouts. *"KOMMST DU!"*

Andy looks at us, clearly preferring to team up with these Yank high-rollers who toss 50 cents around with such abandon, then falls in with his countrymen.

Inside the port building Joe springs into action, delegating all of us tasks. "Bill. Watch our stuff." Bill throws himself across the duffel bags and leans against the wall, grouchy. He may not have slept so great on the ferry crossing.

"You two!" Joe points to me and Eric. "Go line us up somewhere to stay. I'll go check out the town, find a bank." He shakes his cigarette pack. "And some smokes."

We've arrived at the perfect time, after rainy season, when Samui's vegetation is lush and the waterfalls gush, when temperatures range from the 70s at night to 90 by late afternoon. It's gorgeous, an unspoiled paradise, everyone agrees as we're bouncing along in a *bemo* along the island's unpaved main road with no idea where we're being taken.

Eric and I had approached some men at the port, pantomiming we needed someplace to sleep; they'd talked it over. *"Hua Ta Non. Nay Chuan. Pood Ingrish!"* Shortly all this will make sense.

The driver they'd found us pulls up to a compound on the beach in the village of Hua Ta Non, on the island's southeast coast. *"Nay Chuan! Na ma sung farang!"*

There's one vintage-20th century building—a white stucco with high windows and iron grillwork. Everything else around this place is from somewhere in time. The homestead is of weathered-grey lumber, staked up on pilings, with a green- tiled, peaked roof. There are pigs snorting under the house, chickens squawking and strutting out back.

Century-old farm equipment perches haphazardly on an ancient hand truck, sarongs flap on a clothesline.

Joe and Eric love it on sight. For Bill and me, it's a bit harder sell. The place is a far cry from Amat and Muna's immaculate little home, with its electricity and running-water spigot out back, but it's spacious, there's room for all of us, and the beachfront location with Chinese-style fishing junks bobbing offshore is breathtaking.

Mr. Chuan emerges with his family. He and his wife are probably mid-thirties, their son and daughter about 9 and 6.

The kids are in Western-style clothes and flip-flops. His wife's look straddles the fence; barefoot, she's teaming a floor-length Thai wraparound skirt with a white cotton tee-shirt to nice effect, her hair in a fashionable Western bob.

Chuan inclines slightly towards us by way of greeting. "Double room 40 *baht*, singles 20. You eat rice here, each meal, 20 *baht*. Beer, 15 *baht*." He gestures to the well. "You wash out here. WC behind house."

The grandparents come outside, both barefoot and traditionally attired, in ankle-length sarongs. The old man wears a sarong knotted around his head.

"This Mama." Chuan nods at the matriarch. Her eyes dart my way, then down, like a defiant teenager.

"Our house, where you stay." Mr. Chuan leads us up a few stairs across the porch into a windowless common room with wide-planked, sandy floors.

Along one wall there's a wood stove and a slab of timber strewn with woks and pots. The only other furnishings are a table and chairs and framed photo of the King.

Bill and I get the corner bedroom adjoining the porch. There's a full-sized bed, teak table for my clock and radio, tall windows and a cabinet where we can stow our belongings. One perk of traveling as a couple: you get the nicest rooms.

"How long you stay?" Chuan asks.

"Four nights, maybe," Joe says.

"Pay room now, pay later for eat rice."

"*Gin kao*," I say. The Thai word for eat is a phrase: *eat rice*. No meal is served without it.

He smiles. "Ah, *pood Thai?*"

"*Nit noi.*" A little.

"I teach you more."

149

*"Khob kun Ka."* I duck my head to his wife and Mama, the ladies of the house, and say "Hi you guys," to the kids.

The little girl smiles, the boy flashes us a peace sign and grandma scowls, having just deduced she's being put out of her bedroom.

Mr. Chuan later explains that Chuan is his given name, as lengthy Thai surnames are not commonly used, and even close friends address each other with *Nay* or *Nang* preceding the first name. The "mister" is dropped only among family.

The Thai are a formal people. But they are also outgoing. They're hard-working yet fun-loving, proud but humble, an appealing blend of yin and yang.

"INTIRA. DELICIOUS!" Joe tilts his chair back on two legs, slaps his stomach and eyes Chuan's pretty wife.

She points to his empty plate. *"Mak-wa?"*

"No thanks, I'm full." He stands and hands her his plate, towering over her. She tilts her head back, smiles up at him and takes his dishes to the steel washtub on the counter, Joe watching her and Mama watching Joe.

The matriarch strides to the table, glowering, scrapes the leave-behinds onto one plate, then kneels down, grunting, and shoves it all through a chink in the floorboards.

More grunting from beneath the house. The lucky pig who'd been standing under the right hole scarfs up the remains of our dinner.

"They live right below the floor here?" Bill sniffs. "You're kidding."

"Pigs don't actually smell." Eric opens a beer. "If you keep the pen swept out, feed 'em a vegetarian diet and lay lots of straw down there's no odor."

"They put pig manure to all sorts of uses." Joe lights a cigarette with my Zippo.

"You don't say." I hold my hand out for the lighter; it's running low on fuel.

"Be careful with matches and cigarette butts around here." Eric says. "Make sure you spit on 'em."

Mr. Chuan is a small man with a big head for business. He owns his property and grows his own food, minimal living expenses. He puts us up for a dollar a night each. Two meals a day, another dollar apiece; there's nowhere to eat in town. He also owns a generator-powered refrigerator—his ace in the hole. Twenty *baht* a beer, 10 for a cold Coke, a fair price for us, a nice markup for him.

Development will come to Koh Samui in the late '80s. Whether Chuan sells his land or builds it up himself, I've no doubt he'll retire a wealthy man.

At 7 o'clock, Mama lights the lanterns and withdraws, the livestock are hunkered down for the night and we're sitting in near-darkness, sipping beers, listening to the surf pound and coming to terms with the fact that there's nothing to do here nights.

"Get the cards," Bill says, too loud in the quiet. "Whadda you guys play?"

I carry a lantern into our room and find the playing cards, taking a little post-dinner toke of hash while I'm at it. In the next room I hear the guys open more beers. They're becoming boisterous.

A great joke-teller, Bill is basking in the attention of his new audience. While he maintains a steady stream of 'didja- hear-the-ones' that I've already heard, I stretch out on the bed, puff on the pipe and listen to the waves.

Finally he remembers he sent me for the playing cards and calls me to come back out.

We play some rounds of gin at the homemade table by lantern light. "I feel like we're living in an episode of *Gunsmoke*. Mr. Dillon!"

Eric laughs. "This town *is* just like out of a Western. I said the same thing to Joe."

"Yeah," says Joe. "Well, lookit this. We're celebrities."

151

A dozen or so villagers have congregated around Chuan's porch to watch the Americans play cards.

Bill deals, giving them the show they came for.

"Deuce. And-a six. Jack-a-clubs! Possible straight!" He's so clearly a man's man, happiest when surrounded by his buddies. And now that we've found Joe and Eric, it's official. Fun Bill is back.

Or not.

At dawn a bunch of kids are peering through our window-shutters, chanting "YOU! YOU! YOU!"

Bill pulls the pillow over his head. "Get rid of them."

I try to shoosh them. "Could you guys go away and let us sleep?"

They giggle and point to the beach. "YOU! YOU!"

"They're gonna wake the house," comes from under the pillow. "Go play with them. Teach 'em to throw a Frisbee."

"*I* don't know how to throw a Frisbee."

"Get them OUTTA here. It's frickin' 5 AM."

At that a huge commotion breaks out in the hen house. Wings flapping, barnyard noises, bloodcurdling shrieks, then silence.

"Guess we're having chicken tonight," says the pillow.

"Ohmi*god*."

"What?" He sits up. "That chicken lived a much happier life than the ones you buy at the A&P."

I flash on my grandmother taking me to a live Kosher poultry shop when I was little, so I could learn about the old ways; the frumpy Orthodox women wearing wigs, carrying chickens home in paper bags with their heads sticking out—God forbid they should *suffocate*—to be humanely slaughtered at home per the ancient ritual.

I poke my head out the window, flap my arms like wings and shriek. "Buk-buk-buk-buk-buk-buk—bubba GAH!" I've been practicing since Bali.

The children giggle. Even grouchy Bill says, "Not bad, city girl."

After that they follow me everywhere. Down the dusty road to the village, to the beach, through Chuan's barnyard where I'm building a rapport with the pigs, the children are always traipsing behind me. They wait for me outside the outhouse and accompany me to the well, where now a crowd has gathered to watch us bathe.

Joe talks me through it. "They just come the first couple times, till the novelty wears off. Okay? Here goes."

A sarong knotted around his waist, he takes off his wire rims and tee-shirt, reels up the bucket and pours it off into another bucket, which he puts off to the side. Then he completely unwinds the rope and turns the bucket upside down before dropping it down the well.

"You turn it over so it fills all the way up." He reels up the bucket, brimming, douses himself, and swiftly lathers up, hair, chest, underarms. He pulls the sarong apart and soaps up down below, then steps away from the well and splashes off with blasts of water from the reserve bucket.

"All rinsed out." He pulls on his hair to hear it squeak. "Just two buckets!"

The crowd murmurs admiringly.

"All right, your turn. Make it snappy. You don't wanna use any more fresh water than you have to. And you don't wanna show 'em anything you don't wanna show 'em."

I cover my eyes and shake my head. *"Oy yoy yoy."* Everyone laughs, including Joe; the *Yiddische bubbe* routine always kills.

I drop the bucket upside down, reel it up, brimming, and pour it into another bucket, again picturing my grandmother. standing in a 180-degree steam room, boobs down to her waist, pouring ice-cold buckets of water just like over herself without flinching. *Ahh! Good for the system.*

I start from the top, shampooing my hair—briefly allowing soapy runoff to drip into the well to the shouts of the crowd, which to my chagrin now includes not only the children but a number of their fathers—and now I have no choice but to wash my—everywhere else. With the onlookers at rapt attention.

I part my sarong, wash beneath my bosom—big laugh—then squat to wash down south. The crowd goes wild. Now drenched, my figure is clearly outlined beneath the dripping-wet fabric.

Bill appears. "What the hell was that?"

"I had to wash—down there—in front of them."

Bill snickers. "Maybe you should wash first thing in the morning when there isn't an audience."

"There's *always* an audience."

"Hey," Joe says. "These people don't have TVs. This is pretty damn entertaining for them."


LIFE TAKES ON A RHYTHM. After nightfall we hold hootenannies. Eric sings with Bill and me, in 3-part harmony; Joe emcees. He heckles, calls out requests, makes inappropriate remarks to the townspeople, he ogles Intira by lantern light as she glides barefoot across the ancient floorboards, every night is a party. Our act kills; the villagers drink; Mr. Chuan prospers.

At dawn I walk the beach. Gentle waves lap at the shore. Clouds of pink, orange and purple begin to glow. A red pinpoint emerges from the Gulf of Siam, the fishing boats bob. Gulls shriek, like blasts from a saxophone: jazz at sunrise. All is serene in the house of Chuan.

For a while. Then my string snaps. Literally. I'm tuning up and have to jerk backward to avoid taking a sharp wire in the eyeball.

"Which one?" Bill is slouched at the table, shirtlessly awaiting breakfast. "Oh jeez. Your top E? That *really* sucks." He sounds pleased; downright *schadenfreudisch*. "All that entertainment down the drain."

Intira enters wearing a snug pair of jeans that display her cute little behind to best advantage.

Chuan storms in and unloads a choice stream of syllables upon his wife. She sasses back, he shouts her down and now they're in a marital knock-down drag-out in front of four onlookers, our heads swiveling back and forth like at a tennis match.

Intira eventually concedes and returns moments later wearing her customary native attire and a sullen expression.

Chuan ignores her new outfit, as if none of us has any clue why she'd suddenly run off and changed.

"You all go *Nam Tok* today? *Na Muang.* Island biggest waterfall. Hike from the road, good swimming. Beautiful."

"This afternoon, maybe. I have to go to town. Want to come?" I ask Bill. He hasn't been all that active lately.

"Oh, yeah. No. You go on ahead." He's waiting for me to leave so he can rifle my bag for something to read.

So now I'm wandering Na Thon wondering how I'm going to replace a guitar string: *When you have a question no one else can answer, find a Chinese.*

I search the street for Chinese lettering and shortly find some above a doorway leading to what my grandparents called a dry goods store.

Inside, dusty merchandise is stacked high on shelves, sunlight slants through hazy windows; there's grit under my feet.

A bell rings. The shopkeeper greets me in a sing-song torrent.

"Hi. Maybe you can help me?" I point to the empty spot on the guitar neck where an E string should be, say *boi yoi yoi yoing!* and jerk spasmodically.

The merchant giggles, lapses into thought, then brightens. Another outpouring of sound. A finger is raised: *wait here.*

He disappears and returns with a huge smile, brandishing a spool of nylon thread.

"What's this? Fishing line?"

He nods, unleashing an onslaught of syllables that end in his voice rising.

"How much do I need? I dunno." I make twirling motions, showing him how the strings wrap around the pegs.

He unrolls about four feet of line. It's the perfect tension and gauge to replace my busted string. I put it on right there and strum a few chords to show him he'd come up with the ideal solution.

"*Bagus sekali! Kob khun ka.* How much do I owe you?"

Palm in front of his face, vigorous shake of the head. He won't take my money.

Back outside I bump into Andy, the bushy-bearded German who'd been reluctant to follow the others from the ferry.

"*Guten Morgen,*" he says. "Are you enjoying your visit?

"*Ja, sicher.* We're having a great time. You?"

He looks up and down the street and steps closer: apparently not. He's carrying all his gear, a man on the move. "Where are you staying?"

I describe the wooden houses on stilts in the little fishing village from the past.

"Is there room for me in this place?"

Andy integrates seamlessly at the house of Chuan. He loves the location, the rock-bottom prices and authentic setting. He's a notebook carrier, spending most days walking up to people and pointing at things.

"These villagers must think me a queer figure," he'll say, "asking them the name of every flora and fauna and writing it in my notebook." Then he'll pause, waiting for someone to contradict him, and nobody will. He *is* a queer figure.


We hike into the island's mountainous interior, steaming with post-rainy season runoff, where the mighty *Na Muang* courses down towering cliffs of purple granite and spills into a massive pool surrounded by jungle.

"Spectacular!" Eric whips off his Clark Kent glasses and scrambles up the slippery rock, waters cascading all around him. He perches on a ledge, raises his arms gracefully and peers from a terrifying height into the churning pool.

My stomach is doing somersaults. "I can't watch this."

Peeking through my fingers, I see him lean sideways and disappear into the swirling depths.

He surfaces, whips his hair back and forth out of his eyes, takes a few strong strokes to where we're standing and leaps from the water. "Oh, WOW! That was great."

Bill is star struck. "Pretty good!"

My heart's still palpitating. "You could've dived into solid rock."

"You can see where it's deepest from up there." He's like a little kid on a playground slide, racing up to the ledge, high above the canopy, arms raised, shoulders back, chin up, like a ballet dancer, or a superhero, descending to the depth and surfacing again.

We trek back amidst massive granite outcroppings cloaked in virgin rain forest, through lowlands of jungle scrub, until the palms lining the coast reappear.

We reach the road in late afternoon and turn east, sun beating on our backs, sandals scraping in the gravel, making quiet small talk.

*Hot here, away from the Gulf. Yeah.* Some gulls shriek.

*Hottest part of the day. Ja.* Dust clouds from an oncoming pickup. The driver stops.

*"Hua Ta Non? Khuk lang syū kob Nāy Chuan?"*

"Yes, we're the ones staying with Nay Chuan," I say, and we pile in.

"Local celebrities," says Joe. "Like I toldja."


SATURDAY NIGHT AFTER the family settles down and the villagers head home from the hootenanny, Andy draws a bucket from the well and ceremoniously cleans his bong.

"Get the lighter," Bill says. "And some mosquito coils." I go into the bedroom. "Bring the radio," Joe calls.

The lone female, I feel I am being assigned more and more chores as time goes on, while also supplying a disproportionate share of sundries. I grow resentful. I dawdle in response to their instructions.

I theorize that the antiquated surroundings are affecting us, causing us to behave in a manner associated with the time period. Like the time Spock and McCoy get trapped in some planet's past, in the time before Vulcans were logical. Spock starts having emotions. Gets it on with a hot girl who's been exiled there, eats meat, threatens McCoy. I mean look at us. We're drawing water from a well, reading by lantern light, waking with the roosters. The men are reverting to a frontier mentality; womenfolk are expected to serve them. We're in a time warp.

Hua Ta Non is a trap. Beneath this veneer of paradise lurks something sinister, luring unsuspecting young women into a life of servitude.

"We must find the time portal!" I exclaim.

"Huh?" Bill says. "Where's the toothpaste?"

My toothpaste has become *the* toothpaste, of course. "Y'know, the Ice Age one. When Spock gets emotions."

"WHAT?" He's not in the mood. "Awright, fine. The one with the library. Mr. Atoz. What about it?"

*Ah fuck, why bother.* "Never mind."

The next morning Mr. Chuan proposes an Old Samui-style fishing excursion on a longboat, using hand lines. The boys think this is a wonderful idea. So do I. *A day to myself!*

"You do not fish? Okay," says Chuan. "They catch fish, tonight you *cook* fish!"

Great. Now he's bossing me around too.

"Today, shop vegeta*buh*. You know how say Thai for vegeta*buh? Prio wan.* Very good. Children take you."

The village general store is like something out of The Grapes of Wrath. Deep within the time warp.

Goods are shelved behind the counter and customers point to what they want, then the grocer wraps your order in newspaper, exactly the way my mom described shopping during the Depression.

I get home with my Chinese cabbage, garlic, onions, chilis and raw peanuts and the guys with their haul.

"You see what they catch!" Chuan gestures grandly at a tiny pile of puny silver snappers. "Cook in wok," Chuan says. "Mama show you!"

The alpha female of the household strides forward, eyes glittering. *"NAM!"* she barks, winding her hand in the air.

I return from the well with a wooden bucket brimming.

She points to the counter. Fine. I put it down.

She unwraps the groceries, hands me the newspaper, spreads her hands and points to the floor. Fine. I kneel down and spread the newspaper.

Next she hands me a sharp implement and makes short, downward peeling motions.

"You're supposed to scale the fish," Bill says, in a snarky voice I've heard before: *pay the man.*

Okay, this now officially sucks.

Kneeling on a sandy floor, pigs below, the guys, the grandparents and kids above, all waiting for me to scale and gut some frickin' fish, maybe slice myself in the bargain? *Goddamn time warp.*

I was unaware a day's fun for the boys was going to end up with me hunched over Chinese newsprint handling their crappy snappers. "I've never really cleaned fish from – y'know - scratch." Stall for time; play dumb.

Finally Mama emits a slew of harsh syllables, drops to her knees, grasps a fish in one hand, the scaler in the other, takes a few quick, angular swipes, looks at me with malice and rises swiftly from the floor, considering her age and girth. *Your turn, round eyes.*

I look from her, to the men, to the kids, to the fish, gingerly lift one by the tail and attempt to scale it dangling in midair, exactly not how Mama demonstrated.

She lets fly with a stream of syllables. Bill rolls his eyes. "Oh, am I doing it wrong?"

Eric steps up. Possessing the power of flight, he alone has the strength to resist the pull of the time tunnel. He alone has remained a modern, enlightened male who is capable of, and willing to, scale and trim the fish.

I shoot photos of Eric hunched over the little pile of fish on the knotty plank floor with everyone watching. Except Bill and Mama. They're both glowering at me.

But I love the actual cooking part, the old-fashioned implements and exotic ingredients. Under Intira's much more charitable guidance, I oil and temper the wok on the wood stove. She spits at the wok and it sizzles; ready. Smoke rises through a hole in the roof.

I whirl in oil and fish sauce, toss in the garlic, ginger and onions that I've minced on the teak counter with a century-old, razor-sharp knife. When their edges curl I add the raw peanuts and fish, brown and flip them, then add the cabbage, stirring everything continuously per Intira's pantomimed instructions.

Some day when stir-fry is all the rage and everyone's buying electric woks, I'll buy an old-fashioned one just like this and reverently repeat all these steps, spit included, as my own kids watch.


After the family retires, we spoon the fish and vegetables over mounds of rice, crack open some Singhas, fire up the bong and the lanterns and dine by the flickering light and the sound of waves crashing the beach.

"Wow," Eric says. "Dinner's incredible."

"Yeah," Joe says. "Great!"

*"Sehr gut," Andy says. "Danke schön."*

Bill shovels down some rice and takes a swig of beer.

The following morning, I have to count on my fingers to figure out it's Monday. "Weren't we gonna leave today?"

Joe, in sarong and tee-shirt, is going rock hounding. Eric is doing a crossword puzzle in carpenter shorts and a sleeveless tee. Andy, shirtless in Bermuda shorts, long, dark socks and sandals, is poring over a map of Thailand.

Bill pads up the porch steps wrapped in my towel, flicking my Zippo. "This thing's out of fuel."

"We were supposed to leave today," I repeat.

They look around like, *someone just say something?*

Joe ties a sledgehammer around his waist. "Figure we'll pull out around Wednesday."

Yeah, they all murmur. Wednesday sounds good.

"WEDNESDAY?" But we entered the time portal together, so we have to leave together. That's how it works. Besides, I'm not going to Bangkok by myself.

Sensing I am becoming increasingly restive, Chuan suggests I take my camera to Lemai beach, further up Samui's east coast.

"Rocks there, very famous." He steps closer. "Very interesting," he says, with a peculiar intensity.

The beach is exquisite. I climb a bluff overlooking a little cove and snap photos, marveling at the rare solitude. Warm wading pools line the pristine sands of a secluded bay where the very famous, very interesting rocks are found, but it's too far to walk, so I won't learn till decades later why these formations had Chuan so worked up. Web-surfing, I'll find images of the famous rocks of Samui—*Hin Yai* and *Hin Tai,* the Grandmother and Grandfather rocks. They are nothing short of pornographic; anatomically accurate, eerily so. Grandmother is willing, Grandfather able; with a digital ultra-zoom lens, what a prize shot I'd have gotten.

The children intercept me on the way back. Tugging my hands and sarong, they lead me along sandy paths lined by towering palms to the old fishing village. Here the *muezzin* calls the village to prayer from the island's only mosque. Century-old thatched-roof homes are staked up at varying heights according to the family's financial circumstances.

The largest house in the village stands shoulder-high. The one-room shacks with pitch-dark interiors sit only a few inches off the sand.

The kids lead me to one of the humblest dwellings, where a young woman comes out carrying an infant. She looks surprised, though pleased, to see me, and starts rounding up the neighbors. Soon several moms have joined us.

Once we've all bobbed heads and trilled *Sawa-dī tun bāy,* the conversation slows down.

*"Mæ."* Each woman places her hand on her heart, then on the heads of each of her children. They all giggle.

*"Farang."* I place my hand on my own heart. All the ladies giggle. I show them my camera. *"Pob thay?"*

I take pictures of the moms and their kids gathered on the porch, then one of them reaches for my camera and gestures for me to pose with the kids.

I advance the film and show her where to press the shutter, then sit down, swinging one of my little favorites into my lap.

She's about two-and-a-half, full of life, full of the dickens, her black hair bleached almost red by the sun. Her little body bounces joyfully on my knee and that is the moment that I know, that I am certain, that more than being a famous singer, or famous writer, or famous at all, I want children.

What I don't know then, is that even after I have my own little girl, my own little boy, even after I have grandchildren to bounce on my knee, I'll still think about the little girl from Hua Ta Non. She'll come to mind at various times through the years—*she'd be a teenager now. I wonder if she's married? A mother?*

After good byes are said, and the last pictures taken, after I've trudged back along the sand path through the village, and back to the house, I feel a sense of closure. I'm ready to leave this place. I've gotten something I didn't even know I'd come for— a glimpse of the past, a vision of the future.

A little girl in my lap.

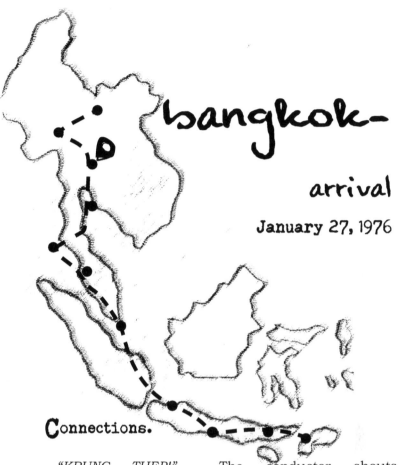

**bangkok—**

**arrival**

**January 27, 1976**

**Connections.**

"*KRUNG THEP!*" The conductor shouts. "HUALOMPONG STATION!" This is it. Bangkok. The big time.

"You sure slept fine." Bill's annoyed I'd been able to fall asleep on the night train from hell. Floors littered with passengers and live poultry, a broken ceiling fan, wooden bench seating at an unforgiving 90-degree angle; third-class rail travel in a third-world country.

"My ass," he moans. "My back!" He's hobbling like an old man, stiff and sore, as Eric and I follow him, stomping our feet to wake them up.

I'd convinced them to leave Koh Samui on Tuesday while the other two had stayed behind, Andy with his eyes on Eric's more comfortable bed and Joe, Chuan's wife.

*You don't think he's stupid enough to...*

*I don't know what he's stupid enough to do.* It was the closest Eric ever came to saying something not nice.

THEY'D SEEN US OFF AT 6 AM, bong billowing, to catch a fast cargo boat back to the mainland Chuan put us onto. It was loaded down with fruit, with no place to sit, so we'd sprawled out across some melons and dozed. This time the all-night voyage took an hour and a half.

Throngs push us through the station onto the street. Heat. Radiating from the pavement through the soles of our shoes, then surrounding us in a force field from which there would be no escape. Fortunately it's the cool season. My Israeli hosts had warned me about this place, and they had lived along the Dead Sea, one of the hottest places in the world.

The noise is deafening, the traffic terrifying, the pollution toxic. Rotting vegetation and all manner of garbage clogs the gutters and canals. Bangkok is a beast to be tamed, an obstacle to be overcome, but it is a city. Somewhere friends will be met, decisions made and errands accomplished, where mail from home, I pray, will at long last be received.

"Where's that diner?" Since Bill read in The Book about the American breakfast served at Bangkok's famous Mitch and Nam's it's all he's been able to think about.

Eric consults a street map. "Looks like it's just a few blocks from here."

As the two of them start walking a blonde approaches me. "Hi. Can I ask you something?" Aussie. "What do Yanks mean by 'blocks?'"

I explain this is the distance between two intersections.

"Oh! Thanks. I wondered. I keep hearing about 'blocks.'"

She's studying me now. "I know you."

I study back. Pony tail, kind of pretty, no makeup, in loose, flour-sack pants and flowing tunic. "Really? I don't think I..."

"You were at the train station. In Jogja."

Nothing. I've never seen this girl.

"You knew this Yank guy...Bill?"

*That* girl? "Were you looking for the Student Travel office?" *In the spike heels and skin-tight black jeans, with acrylic nails and your hair all phoomphed?*

"That was me."

"Wow, yeah! That's right! Hi!"

"Hi." She hesitates. "You know, Bill and I were together after that. For six weeks."

She'd gotten six weeks out of One-Night Bill? Quite the long-term commitment. "No kidding? Sorry I didn't recognize you. You look—you know. Different."

"I suppose so. I packed entirely wrong for this trip."

*Two* things we have in common. "So where's he now?"

"I don't know. He just—took off."

"For home? Back to the States?"

"He wasn't sure. Or didn't say. I don't know." Her voice catches. "I thought we were... a thing."

"Wow, that's a drag." She sounds really down. "Well, as my Gram always says, 'men are like streetcars, another one'll be along in a few minutes.'"

"I guess." She sighs. "But what if you're not ready to get off yet?"

Good point.

Eric turns back, looking from me to Aussie Girl. "You coming?"

"Go on ahead," she says. "Nice seeing you." And she mopes away in her sensible shoes.

MITCH & NAM'S. It's like we stepped into the transporter and materialized on Main Street, USA. Air-conditioned, with booths freshly duct-taped and counter stools on steel pedestals that twirl, and the *pièce de résistance*—a commercial grade, double-burner coffee maker shipped from the States.

"Hi there," booms an enormous black guy with a dish towel over his shoulder. "Leaded or unleaded?"

Bill claps his hand over his heart. "LEADED! Thank you, God." He grabs the menu. "Lookit this. Choice of grits or hash browns, pancakes or toast. Bacon. Every kinda egg."

"And lookit THIS!" I wave them to a Formica table covered in newspapers. "International Herald Tribune, South China Morning Post. Bangkok Post." All in English. "TIME and NEWSWEEK US EDITIONS!"

The three of us fall upon the reading matter with involuntary cries while our host works the griddle.

We hear eggs sizzling, smell bacon frying. Manna from heaven. The big man brings our orders and checks our coffee. "Warm that up for you?"

"We get REFILLS?" Bill sounds on the verge of tears.

"Bottomless cup!" he rumbles. "Just like home."

"Are you Mitch?" I raise my cup to him, the Viet Nam vet who'd settled here when his tour was over to make the world safe for democracy and two eggs over-easy.

"He's not Mitch," Bill says. "He's the Messiah."

For 45 minutes there's only the sound of pages turning and cups being placed on saucers till Bill says "HEY! They found Jimmy Hoffa!"

Eric and I go, "WHAT!"

Bill flashes that devilish grin I find so cute when he's not annoying me. "Gotcha!"

After breakfast we book an American-style motel room in the Sukhumvit district. Eleven bucks night split three ways for a room with flush toilets, private hot-water bath, a pool, two double beds, dial phone and black-and-white TV.

From a fish truck to a cargo boat to a third-class rail car, to dodging foot traffic, trishaws, tuk-tuks, Yank tanks and buses on the life-threatening streets of Bangkok, we've moved 472 miles and 100 years in the last 30 hours.

"Goin' out," Bill yells through the bathroom door.

When they've gone I blissfully shampoo my hair: lather, rinse, repeat. I scrub vigorously, sloughing off millions of dead skin cells the dipper baths have left behind—disgusting—then fill the tub and loll in the hot water—heavenly. The mirror steams up.

When had I seen steam on a mirror last? When had I seen a mirror last? I towel off, open the door, the steam dissipates, and there I am: longer hair, deeper tan, smaller waist. Travel has not disagreed with me.


Standing in line at American Express along with everyone else desperate for word from home, my stomach is churning. There has to be mail. *Let there be mail.*

My turn comes. I step to the window, show my passport, take a deep breath, and ask the clerk and God for my letters.

There are seven.

I save them to read at the pool, sorting through the postmarks while a boom box blasts Bob Seger's *Kathmandu.* Earliest first, or latest? Most recent, I decide. I want to know what's happening *now.*

The latest letter is from my mom, who is "doing as well as she can, given the circumstances." Yellow alert: there are *circumstances.*

Next, a newsy note from my sister, a college freshman. "I hate my roommate. Dorm life sucks."

One from longtime galpals and partners-in-crime, Lucy and Jill dates back to around Christmas. They've moved in together, easy bicycling distance from the apartment along the El tracks my cousin and I share. They're both dating the boys they'll end up marrying, going to lots of holiday parties.

Another from my mom. "I'm starting to feel a little better, though I'm not sure exactly why. It seems that you haven't heard from us in quite a while."

Heart hammering: keep going.

There's a letter postmarked LA my lifelong playmate Ellen typed on an IBM Selectric, a handwritten, monogrammed note from *her* mom, and the last letter, written around Thanksgiving, from my brother. It's laugh-out-loud funny. So I'm laughing out loud. People around the pool are looking at me.

Then the tone changes. "There's something I have something to tell you. Something we talked about before you left."

He's preparing me, not just blurting it out. I cover my eyes, force myself to keep reading. I don't know how it will be phrased, but I know what he's about to tell me.

"Gramma died November 19th."

The homesickness, the months of waiting for mail, the thrill of receiving it, and the certainty it would contain this news all combine with an emotional force I will feel only a few times in my life. As hard as I'd been laughing a moment ago, I am now sobbing. The people around the pool are looking at me again.

Back inside I remember that night of panic in Hong Kong, at the Y, pacing my room, pulling my wheeled suitcase behind me like a dog on a leash. What date was that?

I check my journal. November 19th.

When the boys return late that afternoon, Bill knows some-thing's not right. *What is it?* I've heard that sweet voice before. *Should I come with you to Thailand?*

"I got mail. My gramma died." We just stand there, Bill's eyes on mine filling with tears. He doesn't say anything else.

Finally Eric speaks. "I'm sorry for your loss."

Later, we're stretched out on the bed watching a news report we can't understand. Police in riot gear are lobbing tear gas at Muslim separatists in Southern Thailand.

"That looks like Had Yai." My voice breaks.

Bill looks up from writing a letter. *I'm sorry*, his eyes say, then he rubs my bare leg with his bare foot, like the Empath, from Star Trek, someone who has the power to absorb another person's pain with only a touch.

The next day bossy Bill is back.

I forgot to remind him to buy mailers; now he's run out. I should pick some up. No, he will *not* be accompanying me to the student travel office. We also need shampoo. For a guy who can be so sweet, he sure is a pain in the ass.


There are all kinds of cheap flights to Kathmandu from Bangkok. But there's no air service between Kathmandu and Tel Aviv. I'd have to fly there from India, or hopscotch via Teheran. Neither option appeals.

The clerk and the people behind me are getting restless. I'm holding up the whole line at the Student Travel office, pissing everybody off. I can't decide so I step aside.

They close for lunch. Back on the street, out in the heat. Cars, trucks, buses, motor scooters, tuk-tuks and bicycle cabs dart from all directions. No one stops at red lights, no one signals, everyone speeds. Horns honk, buses wheeze to a stop; someone is always busting concrete somewhere with a jackhammer, the sun blinding and scorching: Bangkok. An assault on all the senses.

I ruminate over a bona fide Coca-Cola at a sidewalk cafe.

Everyone gets sick in India and Nepal. *This Coke is too sweet.* I've already landed in the hospital. Direct flight to Tel Aviv leaves me with 500 bucks for the rest of the trip. *Not fizzy enough.*

169

Ohmigod, is that a phone booth? *You could be a star in Berlin.* I haven't used a phone since Tokyo. *Wish I had someone to call, to talk me through all this.*

And then it occurs to me that I actually *do.*

Butterflies in my stomach, I drop a 5-baht coin and dial the number of the Karen safe house I'd gotten from Peter: fire-fighting, film-making, poem-writing Peter.

The call goes right through, the phone is picked right up and a man trills *"Sawa-dī."*

*"Sawa-dī. Pood Angrit?"*

"Yes," he answers. "I speak English."

Pulse racing, I ask if Peter is there.

"He is!" The man sounds surprised. "Just a moment."

In a second, he's on the line. "Unbelievable! This is the first time I've been here since I got back to Bangkok!"

"So *that's* why that guy sounded so surprised!"

"Yeah. We're actually getting ready to leave tonight. For the hill country."

"Oh." *I* hear how disappointed I sound, can he?

"But not till later. I could come by in a while after I get a few things done—where are you staying?"

I tell him where and return to the hotel to clean up, change, and pray Bill and Eric stay gone.

The agreed upon time comes and goes. No Peter. *He got held up.* An hour later, still no Peter. *He's not going to make it. He must've just had too much to do.* I start tearing up. *At least I got to talk to him again.*

There's a knock. *Damn Bill forgot his key.* I shuffle morosely to the door.

Peter.

"Hi." My voice quivers.

Peter steps through the door, takes me in his arms and we hold for a very long time.

At first the talk comes easy. We fill each other in: my music gigs, inching up the isthmus, the sad news from home; Ernie's departure, Peter's stringing for the Bangkok Post, his leaving tonight for Burma.

Then the Now-or-Never monster rears its head and the talk dies down.

He comes over and stands there looking at me with those icy eyes that make me shiver. He puts his hands on my face, leans down, hesitates for a heart-pounding, confusing length of time—*are you gonna kiss me, or what?*—then finally, *finally,* kisses me, like a lover, not like a friend, and just as I'm expecting the screen to fade to black like in the movies, the love scene hits a snag.

He pulls away, crosses the room, crosses his arms and leans against the desk. "There's someone back home."

"Okay." And you're going home to her. And we'll never see each other again. And you're bringing this up *now?*

Oh, there had been some difficulties before he left, a misstep he *so* regretted. He'd written her a couple weeks ago. Pledged undying devotion and faithfulness. There would be no others. He'd promised. In writing.

A couple of weeks ago. *After* the poem. *After* the hunger, the fever. *After* meeting the viola-playing, corrective-shoe wearing temptress.

He asks if I have someone back home and I say sort of.

"So you mean, platonic."

"No, I don't mean *that*. It's just not…exclusive."

He looks baffled. "I don't get it."

I don't get that he doesn't get it. I'm in *carpe diem* mode here, having once-in-a-lifetime experiences, gathering rosebuds while I may and so forth. I babble something inane about waterfalls and sunsets.

He strikes a professorial tone and stance and starts spewing a bunch of multisyllabic psychobabble from some article he'd recently read. "Men see women as conquests," he lectures. "They fixate on them, objectify them, even objectifying specific parts of their bodies…"

"I have no idea what you're talking about."

What does this nonsense have to do with me, Caryn-with-a-C?

If men have objectified me, that's their problem. No perception of theirs could ever alter mine, of myself.

He tries to explain and I interrupt. "Really. I don't care. About this article you read."

"Okay. But from a feminist perspective, perhaps…"

I put my hand in front of my face, the all-purpose Asian gesture I've adopted that means *No, Stop That, I Don't Know, Shut Up,* because the tide is coming in and the fishermen are shouting and I am caught, and it's now or never.

"I was attracted to you from the moment we met."

He crosses the room in a few long strides, takes me in his arms, hands, breath, lips, bare skin against mine. *Now.*


Once the fever abates and the monster has left the room, everything is relaxed and natural between us. We share a cigarette, we get dressed, we schmooze, then he needs to get back. I brace myself for goodbye.

Instead, he asks me to come back to the safe house with him. How romantic, he wants to be together till the moment he leaves. We flag down a tuk-tuk. "So WHAT WAS THE DEAL WITH ERNIE?" I shout as the tiny three-wheeled taxi darts around in traffic like a pinball.

"HE MET A GIRL." Late afternoon heat and pollution flow through the open cab. Despite their cute names, tuk-tuks are a terrible way to get around.

"THAT'S NICE!" I holler. "Holy FUCK! That bus almost…"

"You're better off if you DON'T LOOK." Peter screams. "A THAI girl. He took her to PHUKET."

A wailing siren stops. "A Thai girl," he repeats in normal tones.

"Yeah. That I heard."

Ernie had taken her to Phuket and everything was great. For a week. Then she robbed him.

"Cleaned him out! Broke his heart. Poor guy changed his ticket and flew home."

"Oh, well. This'll make for a great story some day when he's old and decrepit."

"It's a great story right now!" Peter says. "I can hear the guys at work. 'Man, you SHITTIN' me?' They'll take him for beers. He'll be a hero."

The tuk-tuk turns down a residential street and pulls up to a mid-century styled home surrounded by high brick walls, nicely landscaped, with a Toyota parked out front.

It doesn't look like someplace revolutionaries would occupy. It looks like someplace you'd visit your aunt.

Inside there's a typewriter on a roll-top desk, books and newspapers scattered, dishes in the sink and some mild-mannered men in civilian clothes.

These are the rebels? None of this is what I expected.

I meet Arthur, who'd answered the phone, and then the Colonel—a dapper man of about 50, in double-knit slacks and a sport shirt. One of the top men in the KNLA, the Colonel seems unimpressed with himself and his rank. He'd grown up and fared well under the British. They had educated the Karen, brought them into the mainstream. And for this perceived favoritism, they are now suffering greatly.

The Colonel looks at Peter man-to-man, then casually, like a boyfriend's dad asking me to a family barbecue, asks if I'm joining them to celebrate Resistance Day, at the military base in the jungles of Kayin State—their ancestral home.

I get a flash of the setting of M*A*S*H that proves not inaccurate.

"You should come!" Arthur says. "I'll have you back here next Wednesday. February 4th."

I look at Peter. I thought we'd just be spending a couple more hours together. Does *he* want me to come?

He looks excited. Hopeful. That's all I need to see. I'm going to Burma.

173

BACK AT THE MOTEL I pack up under Bill's supervision one last time while Peter and Eric make small talk.

Bill and I exchange addresses and phone numbers. He walks us to the door, we hug, then he looks at me with this odd expression I can't read. And that's the last I see of him as he closes the door, that strange look in his eyes.

"Your friend was giving me quite the third degree while you were in the bathroom," Peter says. 'Where are you taking her? To some war zone?'"

And even then, I'm so caught up with Peter and this adventure we're going off on that I still don't get it. Only years later will it occur to me that Bill was concerned for my safety.

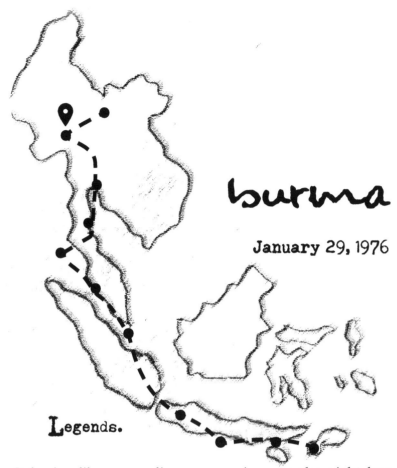

**burma**

**January 29, 1976**

Legends.

It begins like any ordinary excursion—on the night bus out of Bangkok.

Around midnight, we reach a village in the quiet and calm of the Thai countryside. At another Karen safe house, a paneled truck stands waiting. Arthur takes the wheel, the Colonel sits beside him, and Peter and I get in back, in the truck's safety zone: the next leg.

It's the first chill I've felt since that damp, pre-dawn ascent of Mount Bromo. *Four countries and six weeks ago.* We pull on long-sleeved shirts and arrange our gear to keep it from sliding around on the steel floor: my guitar in my lap, Peter's camera case in his, our packs tucked into the smalls of our backs, huddle for warmth, our identically colored hair tangling, and take turns dozing.

175

At dawn we reach Mae Sot, on the Moei River—Thailand's western border. Eyes adjusting to the light, we hop out and stomp around on the ground trying to wake up our feet.

Worst pins and needles ever. "MY BUTT! MY BACK!"

Peter stretches. "You're kind of a *kvetch.*"

*Kvetch. Clutz.* "Say, where'd you pick up..." but his attention is elsewhere. The Major has arrived.

The Colonel's right-hand man is handsome, with an English surname, of military bearing. He wears the officer's uniform of the Karen National Liberation Army—olive-drab trousers and shirt, burgundy beret—and carries two rifles—one for him, one for the Colonel.

"M-14s." Peter looks at me like I should understand why this is significant. I don't. I'm a pacifist; we don't know from guns. We only shoot photos.

Which I do while the men load the longboat that will transport us upriver to camp. They've brought along a couple boy soldiers in civilian clothes. One wears a parka, zipped all the way up, with a bow tied under the hood, like his mother had dressed him.

When all the provisions are secured the Colonel steps toward the center of the longboat, looking no worse for wear through the long night's travel. He raises his pant legs to preserve the crease, settles into the boat's only seat, lays his rifle across his lap, and smooths his hair down to ensure it remains Brylcreemed in place in the windy boat.

The Major sits alongside him on the floor, rifle held upright, and nods at Arthur. We're underway.

Peter turns and I snap his picture to moon over ever after. His brown hair streaked in reddish-gold, his eyebrows bushy and bristling over those startling eyes; craggy features, a drooping mustache, broad-shouldered and muscular, but lean. He smiles. *Can you believe we're really here?* Behind him, an arc of water plumes from the boat.

Upstream the river narrows. The forest is a mix of tropical and temperate; palm trees mingle with pines, banana plants with live oaks, bamboo towering everywhere.

An hour upriver Arthur cuts the motor. We drift over to the west bank, and when we step onto land, we're in Burma.

Among the handful of men clustered on the riverbank there's only one in uniform. They greet their superiors with friendly nods, a Western handshake or two. Nobody salutes. "They're sure laid back. Their commanding officer shows up"—I gesture to the Colonel, who is layering his fashionably long shirt lapels over a striped poplin jacket just like one my dad has—"and nobody's at attention or anything..."

"That's exactly the point," Peter says. "The KNLA is a civilian force." He looks up as the sole uniformed man approaches us. He's about Peter's height, nicely built. A maroon beret tops his thick, shining black hair. His skin tone matches mine: light olive. He has high cheekbones, wide-set eyes, rounder than typically seen among Asians, and handsome, almost delicate features.

"May I help with your things?" He speaks English with little accent and no hesitation. "That's *your* guitar? Perhaps we can hear something later."

Arthur pats him on the shoulder. "Jeffrey plays guitar. He's a virtuoso."

Jeffrey's rifling through a basket. "My #1 fan. Arthur! You obtained the *vital necessities* we discussed!"

"Yes," Arthur says. "Several liters. At an *excellent* price."

Jeffrey bursts into *Satin Doll*, skat-singing into an air-microphone. All the way up the steep stone steps from the riverbank to the base camp, he's snapping his fingers and grooving to the beat—the happy-dance of a man who's gone too long between shots of Mekhong.

The camp is set in a 10-acre-or-so clearing of single-story wooden buildings, a former British outpost in WWII. The building that had served as the central mess is now a barracks for teenage recruits who sleep on straw floor mats, head to toe, with no pillows or blankets. *Uh-oh.*

"Is this where we're going to sleep?" I ask Peter. I was hoping for some privacy. Now I'm wondering how he has characterized our relationship to the Colonel, and to himself. Travel companion and fellow artist with whom protocol had briefly lapsed in a hotel room in Bangkok, or would-be girlfriend, object of affection and desire?

He shakes his head. "No. We're going to be... together."

"How can we?"

He looks at me, eyes icy-hot. "How could we not?"

A ways from the main hall we find a fire pit in front of a three-sided lean-to with hay spread across the ground. "Here." Peter cups my elbow with one hand. "Perfect."

He slips his off his bed roll and unfurls it, unzipping and smoothing the sleeping bag out flat across the hay for us to share. We stack our backpacks, the guitar and cameras neatly in the corner.

Later, true to his Boy Scout persona, he'll prove adept at maintaining a campfire, occasionally rolling over during a romantic interlude to get the logs blazing again before turning back to me. *Now where were we?* He'll ask, and I'll remind him. He'll lean me back gently down in the hay.

"Never mind," he'll say, "let's take it from the top," and we will, because how could we not?

At dinner we're shown to a lantern-lit room with an ornately carved teak table where British officers once dined. We're not the only Western visitors in camp. We're joined by two Frenchmen—Vicente, a stringer for a news agency who speaks fluent English, and Renauld, who doesn't.

Renauld is the handsomest man I have ever seen in person. He has thick, shiny brown hair, brilliant blue eyes fringed in long dark lashes, beautiful features, gorgeous complexion, a physique that's perfection. I force my face into neutral, give him a businesslike handshake and strike up conversation with Vicente, who's lean and wiry-haired, with a broken nose.

The talk is all travel and politics—nothing personal—and Renauld never attempts to join in, though I sense he's following everything.

Dinner every night is a mound of glutinous white rice topped with cooked greens and a pig knuckle the Frenchmen always refuse.

"Do you think they're vegetarian?" I ask Peter later.

"I think they're gay." He gets a mischievous look. "Spies, maybe!"

Nothing in their demeanor, their behavior toward me or each other had given me that impression. "Really?"

"Definitely."

"Or maybe you just can't imagine a guy that beautiful being straight."

"Beautiful?"

"You kidding? Ohmigod. *Unreal.* And those eyes! Even more gorgeous than yours!"

Peter ekes out a weak smile and falls silent. He says almost nothing the whole time we walk back to the lean-to, get a flashlight and walk down to the river. We listen to the flowing current, the jungle night, and then, instead of getting romantic like I thought he'd had in mind, we get into an argument about Israel.

The substance of this argument escapes me but I can imagine how it went: his facts versus my indoctrination. Arabs and Jews had been bitter enemies since Abraham had chosen Isaac over Ishmael; everybody knows that.

Or do they? Sephardic Jews I'll meet in Israel, who'd lived in peace for centuries among the Arabs, will beg to differ. So will historians, who trace the Middle East conflict not to some biblical sibling rivalry, but World War I. But I don't know any of that then. I just know I'm getting the silent treatment.

Back at our shelter Peter builds a fire. If my views have angered him he keeps that to himself. He gently leans me back and we roll in the hay and it seems like all is well.

But the next morning, he's still quiet. I can't figure out what's wrong—can he be taking that disagreement so seriously? The girl back home? Another case of the guilties? It's kind of a standoff. I'm not asking whatsamatter, he's not saying; *either snap out of it or tell me what's wrong*—which he finally does as we're walking back the fair distance to camp from the outhouse along the river.

"Listen. That talk about Renauld being so handsome. 'His blue eyes are even more gorgeous than yours?' That really bothered me. I kind of have a—jealous streak."

I turn to him, smitten schoolgirl heart aflutter. *Jealous? Over me?*

He misreads my expression. "I guess that's a turnoff."

It's the free-wheeling, sex-crazed Seventies. That brief golden age after the Pill but before STDs, when everyone is doing everybody, in couples and groups, sometimes prior to exchanging names. Possessiveness is *so* not cool.

"Turnoff? SERIOUSLY?"

The cold eyes melt. "Maybe not?"

"For *sure* not. See, I was married to this very unemotional guy. Brilliant! Always under control. He never showed—anything. And now here, you—you're..." and I'm crying again, for like the hundredth time since I got to Bangkok.

Peter opens his arms, I burrow against him and we hold until I speak again—against his chest, muffled by the khaki work shirt. "Besides. Renauld's gay."

"And a spy," he says, and we smile at each other, having made up from our first fight.

First and last.

Later, Jeffrey and his guitar pay us a visit at the lean-to. It's a beat-up, piece-of-crap Harmony, with a warped neck and stubborn strings, its body cracked and its finish eaten away by years of jungle humidity. And on this unfortunate instrument from which I'm unable to wring one note, Jeffrey produces rock star riffs that would do Eric Clapton proud.

"Let's hear you on mine." I unzip my case and pass him my Yamaha. "Brand new. Got it in Tokyo."

He smiles at and plucks the fishing-line E string. "What happened here?"

"Yeah, I gotta get a spare set."

"I'll give you the address of a great music store in Bangkok. Oh my." Eyes closed, he runs his fingers up and down the neck of the guitar with a lover's caress. "I haven't felt strings like these..." he does a little bluesy-jazzy warm-up riff.

"Wow, Arthur's right. You're incredible. Where'd you learn to play?"

He shrugs and gives a rueful smile, the same expression I'll see on anyone old enough to remember Burma with a constitution. "In high school, in Rangoon. Once upon a time."

Peter's eyes dart towards his equipment. *I should be taping this*, I can hear him thinking.

Jeffrey's fingers continue to fly up and down the frets, bending notes like I've never heard on an acoustic. "I used to play for all the sock hops."

"Sock hops? In *Rangoon*?"

"Hard to believe? Yes. The girls in their poodle skirts..."

"*Poodle skirts*?"

"Back when we were a democracy. Independent. The Japanese were gone, the British had left..." he shakes his head, lost in reverie. "Susie, Betty, Peggy... dancing in their bobby socks, with their pony tails swinging back and forth..."

Peter asks, "What happened after high school?"

Jeffrey stops strumming.

"Ne Win took over. 1962. Shut down the universities. Disbanded Parliament, started persecuting the minorities. Even the Chinese—his own people!" He passes me the guitar. "Play something."

He's a hard act to follow, but I comply, launching into an oldie I figure he'll know—and Jeffrey joins in. He plays lead to my rhythm, sings harmony to my lead. His voice is true, strong and sweet, our musical compatibility is immediate, flawless, complete. We could've gigged that night.

Arthur wanders over, taking a break from his Radar O'Reilly company clerk duties, followed by several boys, taking a break from I'm not sure what. They applaud when we finish. The boys look awestruck, like I'm Somebody, or maybe they've just never seen an American girl before.

"I've just been telling our friends about the good old days," Jeffrey tells Arthur. "From '48 to '62."

"The 'good old days'?'" Arthur shakes his head. "There was civil war the entire time."

Jeffrey is another incurable romantic.

He teaches us the Karen national anthem, so we can sing along with them on Resistance Day. It's a Western melody in a major key, again, not what I expected. I write the notes and the words in my tiny black loose-leaf notebook. We practice over and over, until Jeffrey is satisfied, then we tape it. Peter says he's going to use it on his sound track.

In forty years, I'm going to wonder if he still has that tape. I'll still have the notebook, and on this same date, I'll find videos of the Karen singing the anthem and discover I can still sing along.

That night we're snuggling in the sleeping bag in the cool of hill country and Peter props himself up on one elbow. "Why do I remind you of Finny?"

We're back to the sailboat, one month, three countries ago: *Have you read A Separate Peace?*

Like the fictional character, Peter is so natural a leader he doesn't even realize it. How his boundless energy and curiosity draw people in, enlisting them in whatever game or cause or course of action he's decided to pursue. He'd led Ernie and Hari and me all over Penang. I followed him to Burma, for godsakes.

"Like today at the river. You wanted to lash a bunch of bamboo poles together and raft upstream, instead of working on your film—just like in the book—how Finny convinced the boys to play that sport he made up instead of doing their homework..."

"Interesting," he says. "Hear that? Finny—raft—Huck Finn"—then he starts going professor on me. "Parallels have been drawn between these characters, you know. The homoerotic subtext..."

"*Again* with the homoerotic..."

He touches my cheek, smiling, pleased, relieved, even, by my answer. "Just thought I'd ask."

He's a bundle of contradictions and conflicting impulses, this man I've followed into a war zone. His thirst for adventure competes with a desire for stability, his drive to achieve is countered by a propensity to goof off, his disgust for the status quo coincides with deeply held traditional values. It all feels so familiar. I could be describing myself.

"The fire's dying down. Should I put it out, or are you..."

"Could we keep it going?" Something else had come up on that boat I want to discuss.

He throws on another log while I smoosh the hay back into a nice soft pile, then ask about the ex-wife I'd been told I resembled.

"Jewish girl." He watches me digest this information. "I knew you were Jewish the minute I saw you."

"You did not! You asked if I could speak English!"

He shrugs. "Conversation starter."

"Uh-huh." *Pick up line.* "Well I knew you were Irish Catholic, right off the bat."

"You did not! You thought we were Aussies, remember?"

"Oh yeah. So anyway. Your ex-wife?"

Peter's break up doesn't sound quite as mutual as mine. His was an open marriage that had taught him an important character lesson: he wasn't cut out for open marriage. But she had liked it just fine. So it ended badly. He'd gotten hurt.

"College kids have no business getting married," I say. "We should've just lived together. That's what my mom said. *Afterwards*. I was like, 'now you tell me?'"

"What, you'd have listened?"

"I don't know." I pluck a piece of hay from his hair. "We were too young. I mean, he was the first guy I ever slept with."

"How old?"

"When we got married?"

"Your first time."

I was the last girl in my group to lose my virginity; this had been a source of embarrassment. We listen to the fire crackle.

"How old?" he persists.

"Nineteen," I mumble.

"Me too! Late bloomers. Anyway... after my wife and I broke up, I was shattered. Then this *adorable* girl falls for me. It was *such* an ego boost. Thing was, she wasn't terribly... um...she was very sweet. Uncomplicated."

"Mm-hmm." *Cute but dumb.*

"Right away, I'm moving in—I shouldn't have. We get these dogs. Then I leave."

"What kinda dogs?"

"She didn't understand, she couldn't accept it. One day she shows up at work while I'm at lunch. I used to go off by myself and like, sob over my ex-wife. Then I'd dry my eyes and go back to being a macho firefighter. It was... surreal."

A masculine man with feminine sensitivities. Oh boy, am I hooked.

"My boss comes and finds me, and goes, 'There's a *really* cute girl here with two great big dogs, looking for you'... it was messy."

The same old story, he wanted the one he couldn't have.

"Wait. So firefighters break for lunch?"

"Smart ass." He elbows me, we both laugh. Then we stay up talking all night: family stuff, some funny stories about my gram. Childhood insecurities, the scariest-ever episode of Twilight Zone, books and movies and music; his documentary, the song I'm working on that needs a better last verse.

"You'll get it." He hums the first few bars few bars: 'Traveling overland, an alien from another time and place. "That's interesting, unexpected, how that phrase resolves. Very cool." He more than just pays attention. He listens, observes, critically, appraisingly, thoughtfully; he more than just gets me, he validates me. He makes me feel as though my work, as though I myself, might become someone of consequence, just as, I am certain, one day he will too.

The fire and conversation wane and we watch the stars. It's a clear, moonless night, like New Year's Eve, and we are as removed from any source of artificial light as I might ever be. I point out Mars. "My favorite planet."

"You have a favorite planet?"

"I'm also partial to Neptune."

'Cause that's where you're from?"

"Smart ass." I point to a big W in the sky. "That's Cassiopeia. And there…" is this possible? I've only ever seen that disc-shaped spiral at the Planetarium. "That's Andromeda," I marvel. "The galaxy next door."

"What? We can see other galaxies with the naked eye?"

"Under the right conditions." *Summer in Superior.*

"Where'd you learn all this?"

"I took a course at Adler Planetarium." *Look kids. You can see the Milky Way.*

"I wanted to take astronomy in college, but physics was a prerequisite, and I think that involves math…"

He snorts. "You think? So, you're not good with numbers?"

"Only when there's a dollar sign in front of them. Then I got heavily into astrology. The real deal, I was doing charts. With a compass and protractor. I bought an ephemeris.

At the Occult Bookstore." *He's gonna think I'm some hippie-dippie flake.*

"I'm into the I-Ching," Peter says.

*Or not.*

"I brought it with me. Ever have your I-Ching done?"

"Yeah. This guy Purple John used to do people's I-Ching's in the student lounge."

"Purple John. Uh-huh. With all due respect—*I'll* cast your I-Ching. Tomorrow. Come up with a question."

We watch a spark shoot from the fire.

"Did you and your ex ever discuss children?" he asks.

"Not exactly." *A little girl in my lap.* "Kinda. I know he wanted kids."

"My girlfriend has two kids. I'm the Daddy-bird." He sounds well-pleased. Another spark ascends. I ask him if he's going to marry her.

He doesn't exactly answer. "I'm going for my Masters in journalism."

I drop it. This is her problem. "I should've majored in Mass Communication. Philosophy hasn't really…"

"So go to grad school."

"Forget it. No more school. I've learned more since I got out of school than I did in college. I learned more in HIGH SCHOOL than I learned in college." I shift around and the hay crunches. "Course I actually attended classes in high school. In college I always cut."

"And you think there's some correlation? Gee, those philosophy courses really paid off!"

"*Again* he's a smart ass." I shove him to the extent possible when two adults are zipped into a single sleeping bag. "Aw crap. Where's the flashlight?"

"You gotta go? Wait, I'll walk you."

"I'm not walkin' no half-mile in pitch black to some smelly outhouse let me OUTTA here…" and he's laughing and I'm wriggling out of the sleeping bag, groping for the flashlight and toilet paper and rushing behind the lean-to and squatting and wondering, if you pee in the forest and nobody hears, does it make a sound? And I decide that it does—the sound of one hand clapping.

THE NEXT MORNING he's hunched over a volume, shaking dice. "Okay, all set up. We're doing your I-Ching. What's your question?"

The question I've been grappling with lately is, where am I going from here?

Existentially, yes, but also from a literal standpoint, when my visa expires…what's next? My onward plans are still up in the air. "Okay. I want to be at the Wailing Wall by March 6th—my birthday." *Mine and Gram's.* "I guess I want to know how it's gonna work out? What can I expect?"

Peter tosses the dice six times, draws a hexagram and interprets the results. "Okay. It's a warning. It could be intended for Israel, or just you. War, or danger. Could be either. It says, take precautions. Be careful." He stares at the hexagram. "But ultimately you will be safe. Or there will be peace. Could be either." He looks up. "So—war could break out while you're there."

Israel is always on the brink of war. "Uh-huh. What else is new?" I grab my towel and sarong. "You coming to the river? I would like to perform my…toilette."

Peter stands watch on the riverbank while I strip and immerse myself in the chill, clear water of the Meoi River, straddling the two countries.

"Where do you think the border is?" I face south and wade to my left; east. "Am I in Thailand now?"

"Maybe." He's shooting the reflection of the landscape upon the water, the warm sunlight angling gently from just above the treetops. I come out of the water and he wraps my sarong around me. I look up, wet hair slicked back on bare shoulders, and he holds the light meter up to my face.

"Perfect."

He steps back and shoots some close-ups of me, and I let everything I feel for him show on my face, glow in my

187

eyes, knowing that, in case he wasn't sure how much I cared for him, once he develops this film, he will be.

That afternoon I have a breakthrough on the song I've been working on, the final phrase that's been eluding me.

*My train whistle's blowing, I've got to be going ~*
*Who knows if our paths will ever cross again, or where?*

Watching him I see I have it, the ending I wanted, the one we wish we could ignore but we're not going to, because that's what we agreed to, that's what we signed on for—a poignant interlude of extreme intensity and limited duration.

"You and Jeffrey are cutting an album today." Next morning he's springing the latches on his equipment cases, taking out professional grade microphone and tape player.

We choose our playlist, decide which keys, where to trade vocals back and forth, and where to showcase Jeffrey, coaxing his soaring, wailing leads from that beat-up Harmony.

Arthur shoots pictures of the three of us sitting cross-legged on the ground of the lean-to, surrounded by equipment, Peter and I in our matching, out-of-style straight-leg levis, both barefoot. Beside me Jeffrey is dashing in uniform, his olive shirtsleeves rolled up, also barefoot, a slanted burgundy beret topping his gleaming black hair.

By the end of the afternoon, we've laid down a dozen tracks or so. Peter plugs in at the barracks and boosts the volume as the boys are filing back in from training.

When they hear the music, they stop and stare at me, wide-eyed.

"Gee, they seem to like it."

Peter answers softly, three words, and the last two are "love you." The initial, all-important pronoun, I miss. Was it *I*—or *they?*

Split second decision; supposing he did love me, he'd never say it, betray the girl back home to that extent.

"That's so sweet," I say, and by his reaction I see I've guessed correctly, sparing us both any embarrassment over what else I might have answered.

We have dinner that night with Vicente and Renauld, flickering gas lamps cast long shadows and jungle night sounds come through the tall windows, speaking softly so as not to break the spell.

Vicente says, "Tomorrow we go to the front. Then Canberra. To deliver a resolution to Kurt Waldheim on behalf of the Karen *résistance*."

Peter straightens up. "You two are planning to confront the UN Secretary General in Australia next week?"

"*Oui*. He'll be there to give a speech."

Peter throws his arm across the back of my chair. "How far is it to the front?"

Jeffrey intercepts us on the way back from the river the next morning. "I've been ordered to the front." His eyes dart behind us. "I am to lead the escort party for Vicente and Renauld." He sounds grim; a soldier with no taste for guns.

"We're coming with you." Peter looks at me. "Okay? We can camp with them tonight, about 10 klicks in, then turn back to the village tomorrow morning. The Colonel and Arthur are taking the boat back to Mae Sot, so Arthur can go back to Bangkok and pick up the mail."

"They have to go to BANGKOK to get mail?"

Peter gives me a look. "What do you think? Someone just shows up from Rangoon with a sack of letters?"

That's just it, I didn't think. It would never have occurred to me that a government, even a dictatorship, wouldn't deliver everybody's mail.

That afternoon our party zig-zags through camp to Mae Ta Wah village and beyond, into *Kayin* State, the wild, remote, disputed piece of real estate the Karen call home.

We trek single file through shoulder-high grasses, alongside massive kapoks with huge roots exposed, flowering bushes and trees choked with woody vines Tarzan could swing from, and bamboo, thick and tall, everywhere we turn.

A couple machete-bearing uniformed troops take the lead, followed by two trainees in civilian dress, each carrying a massive straw basket loaded with supplies. Jeffrey and Arthur stay in the middle where they can supervise the boys while keeping their four Western charges in sight.

If not for the cicada-din this would seem a peaceful setting, but the insects are in that late-afternoon frenzy when they screech unceasingly, then fall weirdly silent at the exact same instant, leaving a ringing in our ears that will be drowned out only when the cacophony resumes.

In the midst of all this racket Jeffrey signals us to stop. "Everybody roll down your sleeves! Tuck your pants into your boots! Leeches! They can attach without your knowing and you feel perfectly fine until you collapse from blood loss." He rolls his sleeves down smartly and buttons the cuffs, watching our faces.

"Just kidding. Most people notice blood stains on their clothing before actually losing consciousness."

While we're stopped, he gives the boys some instructions in their native Sgaw dialect. They smile and start rustling through the packs, eventually coming out with a couple fistfuls of—what the hell? They're heading into battle smoking cigars?

I'd never imagined that anything about going to war might be considered fun, but here they are, gleefully lighting up.

Jeffrey passes me one, hand-rolled, about six inches long. "Try it. This is a cheroot."

I get a vision of my grampa clipping the end off an El Producto, handing one of us kids the ring, then slowly masticating it into a nauseating pulp through the course of an evening. "No, thanks. Really."

"This is like no cigar you have ever seen," he says. "It has a filter—look." Some shreds of corn husk have been rolled up and inserted in one end.

"Besides tobacco, spices and aromatics are mixed in. Very tasty. Women smoke them."

"Take it," Arthur advises. "Cheroots are effective in warding off leeches."

"*Again* with the leeches?" I whine. "Will you guys cut it out?" I take the cigar while the men laugh. It's all very 5th grade, boys taunting girls with creepy crawlies at recess, except the boys are rebels in the middle of a civil war and recess is taking place in a rainforest in central Burma.

I find the cheroot much to my liking. It's mild and flavorful, and the corn husk filter prevents the end from becoming slimy. When we've all lit up, our column starts moving again in single file. I hoist my pack up on my back, button the cuffs of my flannel shirt, clamp the cigar in my teeth and set off to follow the soldiers.

"Ohmigod," I say to Peter. "If my mom could see me now."

He turns, smiling, holds his hand out to steady me over a tree root, then raises it to my cheek, like he's reading the light meter.

We continue in single file through about six miles of dense forest, always within earshot if not view of each other. No strangers to this kind of terrain, Vicente and Renauld keep a brisk pace up front with the troops. Every so often the cicada hysteria tapers off, allowing snatches of the boys' conversation to drift back. Jeffrey chuckles, turning to Peter and me.

"They're talking about how handsome Renauld is." Suddenly he stops short and raises his hand for silence: ahead of us, the men have stopped talking. We hear twigs snapping underfoot.

Jeffrey strides resolutely forward and motions us to follow. When we catch up to the others they're congregated in a small clearing. We all stand silent and still, our eyes fixed in the direction of the sound.

Dappled sunlight peeks through the canopy, creating a natural paisley of dark and light that so closely matches the tattoos covering every inch of the man in our path that not until his eyes move do I realize there is a naked human standing among the trees.

He's holding a spear.

Beside him stands a Western standard-issue missionary or journalist type with a rifle over his shoulder.

I feel smoke in my eyes and remind my hand to remove the lit cheroot from between my clenched teeth.

Naked Spear Guy isn't actually stark naked, he's wearing a G-string woven of—I don't want to know. Different kinds of hair. He's in an elaborate headdress of bones and feathers. Long, pointed tusks protrude from each earlobe, and across his muscular chest hangs a necklace of many sorts of teeth.

His eyes calmly sweep the scene.

He takes in the three white men, the Karen teenagers, the uniformed soldiers, and finally, the curiosity that appears to be a young Western female—plaid flannel shirt knotted at the waist, blue jeans tucked into hiking boots, hair in a messy bun secured by a leather barrette, smoking a cigar—and he smiles.

Jeffrey bows slightly, gestures for them to take the path and the two continue on their way. Everyone's quiet.

When we're well beyond them and can't be overheard, one of the boys turns to Jeffrey.

"Naga?" He whispers, like a kid hearing a scary story. Jeffrey nods. "Naga. That was a headhunter."

The sun is just above the tree line when we reach our stopping point, where a footpath intersects a rapidly moving stream. We all drop to our knees, splash the cool, clean water in our faces, and drink in enormous gulps, gasping.

Peter and I return to the stream at twilight. We peel our grubby clothes, then plunge in, submerged in the chill water.

"Later," he murmurs, arms around me, warm breath on my cold, wet ear.

"With everybody surrounding us?"

"Mmm-hmm. Think about that. I will be."

The promise of darkness hovers between us for a moment and then he's all business—the fading light and jungle sundown chorus will make for great footage as the men set up camp.

We return to find the boys clearing some tall grasses around the perimeter of the site. One of them cuts a stalk of bamboo neatly into lengths, slicing below each joint to make drinking cups for everybody. The troops are digging a hole for a campfire, chattering and smoking cheroots.

Arthur produces a huge, battered tin pot of pre-cooked sticky rice wrapped in banana leaves, vegetables and sauce that will be warmed over the campfire for our dinner. Jeffrey searches his own pack.

"Hah!" He's waving a bottle of Mekhong whiskey. "Now! Let's get...in the *mood...*" he croons, grasping the neck of the bottle like a hand-held mike. I'm relieved to see him so light-hearted again after his grave demeanor this morning: *I've been ordered to the front.*

We hold out our bamboo cups and he pours shots all around. We toast each other. We toast the Naga headhunter, we toast the rebellion.

It's all very convivial, everyone laughing in the firelight, nobody knowing this conflict will continue for decades to become the world's longest-running civil war, and that even as peace negotiations drag on between the Karen National Union and Burma's elected government, the villagers of Mae Ta Wah will remain at the epicenter of armed hostility, in constant peril.

After dinner, with Peter off filming and everyone settling in for the night I keep Jeffrey and his bottle of Mekhong company at the campfire.

He suavely tilts the bottle towards me.

I give the *'none for me, thanks'* signal, just like we're in a cocktail lounge, then he pours himself a shot.

"So tell me—"sipping whiskey from the bamboo stalk. "What have you learned from your travels?"

"Great question."

He nods. "Cigar?"

"No thanks." I wag my finger at him. "You're a bad influence."

He likes that. "So?"

"Wow. Where do I start. Geography, history, language, religion. All these people and places I never heard of..." I glance at him, handsome in the firelight. "But that's not what you meant..."

"No. I mean—the significance of it all? The lesson learned? From all...this?" He indicates our surroundings, as removed from all that is familiar to me as I've ever been.

I button my flannel shirt in the chill. "I've thought about this a lot. When I started out—in Tokyo—all I could see was how different everything was. The contrasts. But now what I notice most is how we're all so are similar."

How might such talk come across to someone who's lived his life as an outcast? That doesn't occur to me.

"Similar. How so?"

In Surat Thani I'd shown a bunch of women—fruit peddlers—pictures of my family. Looking from me to the photo, they'd correctly identified everyone: *sāw, Mæ*—sister, mother. *Phī chāy.* Brother. I tell him about that.

Then the head peddler, the alpha female, pointed to my grandmother, looked me in the eye and said *Mæ khung mæ.* Mother's mother. Right then I knew for certain my grandmother had died. That part I don't mention.

"We all share such a common frame of reference. The whole human family thing, you know?"

He sips his whiskey, a man who has been cast out of the family.

"Then...meeting you. I mean, we come from *really* different backgrounds, and here you are..."

"Finishing your sentences." We both laugh.

"But you've gotten impressions," he says. "Of all the different types of people you've met. Noticed the distinctions"—he scowls, and pours more whiskey—"that are of such life-and-death importance to us?"

"Physical differences, sure. But character traits, I really can't say. I never know if people are acting regular around me. The way they'd act if I wasn't there."

Jeffrey's cigar glows in the darkness. "You know what? I will have one."

He hands me a cheroot, and his to light it.

"One thing I learned is, nationalities over here are all kind of...made up. Like, there's no such thing as 'Indonesian.' There's Balinese, Javanese, Tengger, Batak. Whatever. You know how many languages they speak in that country? That's not really a country?"

"Hundreds. It's the same throughout Asia. Burma has dozens of distinct ethnic groups, ranging from me—an English-speaking, Christian Sgaw Karen, to the Paduang— those long-necked women who wear brass coils around their throats—to that Naga man this afternoon." He blows a smoke ring. "That was a very unusual sighting. They rarely venture this far east."

"The headhunter? Oh my God. That was the strangest human being I've ever seen."

"I daresay he thought the same of you." He tosses kindling on the fire. "Headhunting was banned in '62. But no one's really sure if it's being enforced." We watch as the tinder flames.

"See Westerners, we're into the whole 'geography is destiny' thing." *Location, location, location. He won't get that.* "Where we're from—where our families are from—the neighborhood we grew up. Over here, when we meet, the first thing we ask isn't 'what's your name?' It's 'whereya from? Whereya from?'"

He nods. "Here, among migratory people, political boundaries are arbitrary. Ethnicity rules. And when ethnic borders don't conform to the political ones—oh dear. That causes quite a bit of strife. That causes—this." He gestures to all the men. "You said...people don't act...'regular' around you. Always? And how *do* they act?"

I hold out my bamboo for a shot. "Okay. Either they act condescending—which pisses me off—or subservient—which gives me the creeps."

He sighs. "Ah yes, the pecking order."

"Except the Thai. They're different. They're friendly, they're curious. But they don't seem to have this East vs. West complex like everyone else."

"Because they've never been colonized."

"Exactly! Thanks to Rama IV and Rama V—Mongkut and Chulalongkorn. They were like: 'The round-eyes are here. Let's learn to play their game.' Rama IV corresponded with Victoria. Lincoln. As their peer. Chulalongkorn graduated from Oxford."

"You're quite knowledgeable about the Thai royal family. Let me guess. You've seen The King and I."

"Know all the songs by heart. But I read an actual biography of Mongkut."

"Then you know he looked nothing like Yul Brynner..."

"So *you've* seen it."

"Many times. In Rangoon, back when it was the cinema capital of Southeast Asia."

He straightens up and starts belting out the King's big number—*When I was a boy, world was better spot! What was so was so, what was not was not!*

I join in at the chorus: *Some things nearly so, others nearly not.*

"Jeffrey!" Arthur yells. "No more!"

"Singing, or Mekhong?"

"BOTH!"

We hear scattered laughter, then more murmuring and chuckling around the campsite as this exchange is translated into French and Sgaw.

I lean towards Jeffrey, starting to feel the whiskey.

"Truthfully? I think every minority believes they're superior to everyone else. This course I took in college, the whole class was black except me and this other guy. So I tell them my theory, then say, 'You guys feel that way, right?

That you're better than white people?" They're lookin' around, going 'um...well...uh..' Finally one guy goes, 'HELL, yeah!'"

No response.

"You feel that way. I'm sure of it. Don't you believe that the Karen are physically, intellectually, morally superior to all these other tribes?" I take his silence for assent. "Believe me, I get it. Look at my own ethnic group. We call ourselves The Chosen People."

Jeffrey's back goes rigid. "You're...a JEW?" He stares at me intently like people do when they're looking for our horns. "I've never met a Jew before." His hand, holding the bamboo cup, seems frozen in mid-air. We watch the burning cheroot ends glow in the dark.

"You and I may have more in common than we know," he says. "There are legends."

Crickets chirping, the stream running in the background, then twigs snapping.

"Don't put that whiskey away yet." Peter settles in beside us and Jeffrey pours him a generous shot.

He raises his bamboo shot glass and knocks it back. "What've you been talking about?"

"Everything," Jeffrey says. "Ever see The King and I?"

"So THAT'S what you two were singing. Are you guys drunk?"

"It was banned in Thailand, you know," Jeffrey says. "The King was depicted as a buffoon—a savage who thought the earth was flat—when in fact, he was a renowned astronomer. He died of malaria he caught while viewing a solar eclipse he had correctly predicted."

"The King was an astronomer?"

"A great reformer," Jeffrey says. "Very progressive. The Thai call him 'The Father of Science.'"

Peter holds out his cup. "Wow, talk about irony."

"He did have all those wives though. That part wasn't made up. And 82 children. After 27 years of celibacy!"

He pours himself another splash. "So maybe there's still hope for me!"

"I think I felt a drop," I say.

We wait a few seconds, then we all feel it. The temperature falls, the rain picks up, we say good night.

Peter leads me to a secluded spot he's picked out, under a stand of bamboo.

"He's a beautiful man," I say.

"He is." Peter unrolls the straw mats the boys packed in for us. We just stand there in the drizzle, till at last he smooths the sleeping bag out over the mats, unzips it and turns a corner down neatly, like at a ritzy hotel. "Climb in." I wriggle into the sleeping bag, not wanting it to start, because once it does it's going to have to end.

"Well?" he finally whispers. "Aren't we gonna?" And I turn to him, because how could I not.

We make love for the last time in total silence. I'm choking back tears and raindrops are trickling from bamboo leaves: I'll never forget this night, this place; *these people, this man, this feeling* then the wave, the current, running between us, Peter's warm breath at my ear, *yes,* he whispers. *Yes.*

After he dozes off, I lie awake, snuggled against him in a single sleeping bag. *I never expected to end up here.*

The rain is mild, but it lasts all night, dripping on the sleeping bag. I hardly sleep, but I must have for a little while, because I dream that I am home.

I'm standing in line with my brother and sister at a travel agency. The line is long, the wait excruciating, everyone else in front of us is very old, finally our turn comes and an old man in a brown suit steps up to the counter in front of us. *Can I have some help,* he says, and his voice is so kind, so gentle, that even though we've been waiting forever, we give him our place in line.

While we're hiking back to the river, I'll tell Peter this dream and he'll say it's about death, and I'll agree. Though only much later will I realize just how right he was, when I'll remember, at age six, asking my mom what Daddy was wearing in that box in the ground, and that she answered, *his brown suit.*

But right now it's sunrise and we're all shaking rain off the sleeping mats. We wash at the stream, fill our canteens, pack up. We shake hands with Vicente and Renauld and wish them godspeed, then Jeffrey tells us a small party of rebels passing our group gave him some disturbing news.

"There are gun reports from the front." He looks grim.

"How many guns were reported?" I ask.

Peter and Jeffrey look at each other like I just made a dumb girl remark.

"Report means 'gunfire.' Peter says. "He means there's shooting at the front."

So 'report' means gunshot. And a 'troop' consists of just one guy? It seems there's a special war language—one I have no interest in mastering. It's the language of people getting killed. And for what? Because they choose to wrap coils around their necks, turbans around their heads, or leather straps around their wrists?

I suppose I'm oversimplifying, and I do believe there are ideals worth dying for, I just don't think any war has ever been fought over them.

Jeffrey straightens up and turns to his men with cheerfulness and resolve. The Colonel promised him leave in Bangkok after his stint at the front and he'll call when he gets in. "Leave word with Arthur," he says. "I'll see you in a week."

Then they head west, into harm's way, and Peter and I turn back east, where we will be safe. Where we will say goodbye.

Arthur directs us to a footpath that eventually widens to a gravel road leading to the next village south of Mae Ta Wah, giving us a shorter walk and some time alone.

Mid-morning, a *bemo* pulls up carrying a pretty young woman in traditional Karen attire and her infant, who looks about 8 or 9 months old.

The baby looks from me to Peter, then starts to wail. The young mom turns her palms up, embarrassed we'll think our alien looks are scaring her baby.

I gesture to her: no offense taken. "She's adorable. Hi, sweetie," and Peter says, "Cute baby. Very alert."

The young woman smiles, not understanding our words, but that they are well-meant.

She jiggles and pats the little one, who finally simmers down, with a watchful, uneasy expression.

Killing time in the village before the longboat arrives, we wander into the village store, perched high on the riverbank. With a counter and shelving that once might have been stocked with goods, it's now almost empty, selling strictly black- market items, whatever can be brought in from across the river.

We buy a couple bottles of warm, sweet soda pop from a man who looks to be in his sixties, taller than the others, but with their characteristic light complexion.

"Will that be all?" he asks.

Everyone in the store laughs. There's nothing to buy.

I ask if I can pay in *baht*. "Certainly. All foreign currencies are welcome here." More laughter.

He takes a cigar box from under the counter with some scant change in it. I notice *baht* and Malay *ringgit*, a few marks and shillings, and some very unusual-looking coins I've not seen before. They're all different shapes, even triangular, with holes stamped in the center and embossed with an alphabet that is definitely not Thai.

"What are these?"

He snorts and scoops them up. "You want them?"

I shake them in my hand. They weigh practically nothing. I try to give him more *baht*, but he waves me off. "Keep it all. That's the old Burman currency. From— before. With these you can purchase...nothing!"

Everybody laughs again, finding these desperate circumstances highly amusing.

Outside I comment it's surprising to find English so widely spoken out here in the middle of nowhere.

"That's part of the problem." Peter reaches for the soda bottle. "The British took the Karen under their wing.

"They'd been oppressed for centuries, getting killed for things like... learning how to read. The Karen fought with the British to run the Japanese out. The Burmans sided with Japan. Till they started losing. Then the Burmans switched sides."

He takes a swig of pop and winces. "Sad thing is, it could have worked out. After the war, when they were transitioning to self-rule, a Christian Karen ran the army. Aung San, a Burman, was appointed prime minister. He wanted to unify Burma. He gets assassinated and that's it. The Karen were fucked." He sighs, reaching for my hand.

"Now, so is everybody else. Come on. We better go find some shade."

We lean up against a tree and Peter cues up our album on the tape recorder. People approach, we wave for them to come and listen; when a group has gathered, Peter plays the Karen anthem he'd taped on Resistance Day, and everyone joins in.

Not long after he points upriver. "See that water plume? That's the long boat. We'd better get our stuff together."

I look at him, fighting for composure. This is it.

Peter lays a hand on my cheek. "Hey. I'm seeing you back to Mae Sot."

On the river I pull myself together. We busy ourselves with Peter's submission to the Bangkok Post about Vicente and Renauld's plan to confront Secretary General Waldheim. He composes, I edit; *your spit of polish, my bits of glass.*

The finished piece is better than either of us could have produced on our own.

In Mae Sot we walk through an outdoor market along the river. What looked like a little backwater town five days ago now seems a thriving metropolis, full of things to do and see and buy, in a country where people are free to come and go.

"This place looked like Nowhereland when we got here from Bangkok. Now it's Times Square."

He nods. "It's all a matter of perspective, isn't it?"

Perspective is something I'll be ever mindful of, in future creative endeavors, my career, my travels, and especially in my family life.

The perceived injustices my parents subjected me to I"ll visit upon my children, to keep them safe, to shape them into the accomplished adults they'll become.

We give our kids the car keys; from our parents, we take them away.

These observations are in no way unique or original, they are universal. Still, they always come as something of a revelation to us all.

But back in Mae Sot, I'm just trying to get through the next few minutes.

"Guess we better go." Peter notices Arthur signaling from the far end of the market. "They're ready to leave."

We join Arthur and the Colonel. I thank them for their hospitality. I tell Arthur to have Jeffrey look me up at the Federal hotel in Bangkok. I wish them success in their fight for freedom.

They wish me safe travels and leave to load up the boat. Now this really *is* it.

Peter and I put our arms around each other. We look into each other's eyes and he raises his hand to my cheek, like he's reading the light meter.

He says, "my train whistle's blowing, I've got to be going," then leans forward and we kiss softly, just like in Penang.

Peter slides his hands down my arms, grasps my hands and raises them to his lips. Then he turns to walk away and doesn't look back and I watch him till he disappears, my friend, my love, my kindred spirit.

# bangkok–
## return
**February 4, 1976**

Omens.

I stumble away from the station into the dawn, into the noise and crowds, the pollution and blazing heat that say morning has broken in Bangkok.

Sad to leave Peter, outraged over the situation in Burma, uncertain as to what lie ahead, a couple jammed beside me in a double seat and their kids lying beside us in the aisle, I'd put my arms around my guitar and rocked it over hundreds of miles of bad road.

Mike and Lin are supposed to be at the Federal, but I can't bust in on them at this hour, assuming they're even there. Everyone's plans always changed on the road. I'd never been anywhere I thought I'd be on the day I thought I'd be there. Why would they?

But I have nowhere else to go.

So I sling the guitar over my shoulder and soldier on, backpack bobbing behind me, boots covered in Burma's mud and dust, jeans stiff from wading through streams, wearing the same tee-shirt I've been in for three days, I stride into the business center of Bangkok's most exclusive hotel to clean up and change.

Now cool and composed, steeled for disappointment, I go to the Federal to ask for Lin. I approach the front desk and the clerk's face brightens, like he's been told to expect a Yank girl with a guitar.

She answers my knock in a batik sarong, Orphan Annie ringlets framing her freckled face, the adorable girl next door. "Just you?" she asks. "No Bill?"

"No Bill." My lips start trembling.

"What happened?"

"Peter." My voice breaks, she pulls me in and closes the door, and finally, safe with Lin, I let myself lose it.

Finally, bored of my sniveling, I start looking around the room. "Where's Mike?"

She hands me some tissue from the nightstand.

"In Singapore, getting his last paycheck and the rest of his stuff. You can stay here tonight, there's an extra bed." The place looks out of my price range. "It's already paid for," she says.

I'm gonna start crying again.

"Oh God, are you going to start crying again?"

"You should've seen me the last time I was here." I ball up the tissue. "I finally got mail from home."

"Your gramma?"

"Yeah. She died while I was in Hong Kong. This whole time I kept writing her letters and they were getting forwarded to my mom. Oy God. My poor mom." I wipe my eyes, then my face.

"Hot out already?"

"Brutal. I practically fainted walking here from the President. They got real nice bathrooms."

"You were walking? Or you were being chased?"

Now we're laughing, remembering our New Year's Day escapade, and I'm OK after that.

Back out on the scorching streets, we're almost at Mitch & Nam's when my knees buckle. Traffic, pollution, heat, nothing to eat, everything is swirling like in the scariest Twilight Zone ever... *I'm going down...*

Heat getting to you? Lin, sounding far away, her hand at my elbow: Bend over. Breathe. Just breathe. It'll pass.

I inhale, filling my lungs with hundred-degree toxic fumes, grip my knees and wait for the spinning to stop. Bangkok. You have to kind of get acclimated.

Over two sunny-side-up and a side of hash browns I explain how Bill and I had started getting on each other's nerves. The missed bus, his opium, my traveler's checks; ferrying with Peace Corps Joe to Koh Samui, where he'd become increasingly irksome, always bossing me around, mooching things off me, my toothpaste, my shampoo. I pour some more syrup over my pancakes. "My *towel*, even."

"*Ewww*." Lin drains her coffee cup, gazing worshipfully at Mitch as he refills it. She'd been no big fan of Bill's personal habits.

"I became his little Gal Friday, 'Remind me to do this, go get me that.' Really pissed me off."

She reaches for the syrup. "Yeah, I wouldn've stood for that. Then what?"

I tell her then what. Peter, the longboat to Burma, the Karen camp, Jeffrey. The trek into the jungle, the tattooed man with the tooth-necklace. By the end, her face looks like mine must have after she told me about her week in Kabul disguised as a boy.

"Wow. WOW." Lin shakes her head, and that's when I know I've arrived, that I too, am now a Traveling Woman.

Later, while we're stuffing an actual washing machine at an honest-to-God laundromat, she asks whether Peter and I are planning to stay in touch.

"We exchanged addresses." I rip open a packet of Rinso. "His was care of his live-in girlfriend."

She closes the lid and we're quiet for a moment, delighted by the sound of an automatic washer filling with hot water. "But why would he risk it? Your letter coming to her house? If he really didn't want..."

"Oh, it was the 'let's send each other pictures when we get home' conversation, when you know you never will?"

I tell Lin about the rebound girl he'd moved in with while he was getting over his divorce, how he'd broken up with her and she'd come chasing after him at work.

"What? In the middle of a forest fire?"

"Yeah, that part I wasn't clear on." I watch her smooth a pair of cut-offs from the dryer. "So anyway. She comes after him, and then she's just like this *nuisance*. I don't want to be *that* girl. I want to be that *dream* girl. The one he'll always remember and wonder about. You know?"

"Like he'll always be for you." She knows.

We wander Bangkok's streets for the rest of the day, ducking under awnings for shade when we can find any. We take photos of people shopping the street stalls. In front of one a woman is stretched out, fast asleep on a piece of cardboard and everyone sidesteps her, careful not to disturb her nap on the burning sidewalk in the business district at high noon; the Thai are considerate that way.

Which is why I'm so surprised at what happens next. Someone hits me. A wizened old man reaches through the bus window and whacks me, hard and sharp, across my shoulders.

Lin comes over. "What the HELL?"

"I don't know." The bus pulls away in a cloud of diesel fumes. "ASSHOLE!"

A couple of saffron-robed monks within earshot purse their lips and turn away, like I was the one out of line.

"He wouldn've tried that if there was a man standing here with us," Lin says.

The next day I find an incredible deal out of Bangkok to Amman, Jordan on Alia, the Royal Jordanian airline. The catch is, I will have to cross into Israel from Jordan.

This gives me great pause. American Jews can move freely in countries where Israelis aren't allowed but—do I dare? *They'll know. My ethnic surname will give me away.* Wait a minute. Give me away? *Shame on you,* says one little voice. *You're trying to pass?*

*The clock is ticking,* says another, *and your supply of Traveller's Cheques is dwindling.*

El Al to Tel Aviv, $600; Alia to Amman, with onward stops in Athens and Madrid, unlimited stopovers permitted, $282. If crossing the East Bank proves too risky, I can just fly through to Athens and grab a cheapo flight back to Tel Aviv.

I neatly detach and sign six 50-dollar travel checks. *Interesting,* continues the voice. *The airlines have the same name.* El Al and Alia both mean "to go up," in Hebrew and Arabic. I take this as a good omen.

But it ends up just being an omen.

I visit both embassies over the next few days, determined to do the homework this time.

The Jordanian official is charming and accommodating. Yes, he purrs. Many travelers enter the Holy Land by way of Amman. Trains run from the airport to the Allenby Bridge, a short distance, but I should allow two hours. He stamps in my passport a generous 30-day visa that will cover exit and re-entry.

The Israeli official is curt and disagreeable. Yes, he snaps. Americans can cross back and forth between Jordan and Israel; even...*American Jews.* Would I like the Israeli visa in my passport? Or just on a transit card, so there will be no... *difficulties* entering other Arab countries?

"Stamp my passport."

He nods; I have answered correctly. "That border has been quiet of late."

207

Then I go to the Hotel Malaysia to meet up with Allan. My gut says he won't be there, and he's not. So much for playing the clubs in Bangkok.

But thumbtacked on the hotel bulletin board, high up in a visible spot, there's an index card addressed "Music Maker Caryn" in his precise, artistic hand. Allan has been here and gone, his plans have changed. Even so, I'm touched that he's left word. I respond below, that I have been here and gotten Allan's message, when another card catches my eye.

It states: *Amman is a hole. The only good thing about it is going to Israel.* This seems to support the Jordanian's claim that crossing into Israel from Amman is common practice, so I erase any further doubts from my mind and resolve to deplane in Jordan.

Later, though, I'll wonder whether I'd been purposely misled, or the polite man at the embassy simply wanted to seem welcoming and meant no harm. No trains ran from Amman to the Jordan river. The visa I was issued would get me to the East Bank, but not across. The I Ching's message was intended for me personally, not the State of Israel, and it would prove prescient. I did face grave danger, but ultimately, I was safe.

In the following days Mike and Lin and I visit the palace, the golden wats featuring the Buddha in every imaginable mood and pose, the Floating Market. We take a boat ride on a stinking canal, then I get restless and expenses start mounting so I decide to go to Chiang Mai after all.

They see me off at the bus station, armed with instructions: where to stay, what to do, and when to be back—Friday, February 13th, because they are flying home the next day.

"Valentine's Day." Lin smiles up at Mike.

He rocks his broad shoulders. "Yep. You git back to see us off now, y'hear?"

I watch them till Mike's lanky form can no longer be seen above the throngs. *Damn I love those two.*

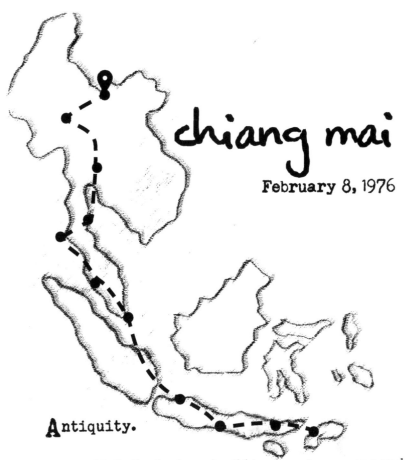

# chiang mai

**February 8, 1976**

**A**ntiquity.

Chiang Mai's fresh air and mild temperatures are a god-send after Bangkok.

I pass through a towering 700-year-old gate into the Old City, which is surrounded by a moat that had held intruders from Burma and Siam at bay in earlier times, when Chiang Mai was a kingdom unto itself.

Now it is a tranquil place, where tribal populations are allowed to maintain their traditional way of life, weaving silks and tending poppies in their distinctive styles of native dress, going about their business as they have for centuries. The Meo have settled here, the Hmong, and the Yao, various branches of the Karen, including the Paduang of neck-coil notoriety. The modern-day Kingdom leaves them in peace.

Ex-pats are drawn here as well. Germans own the café on the square where the town's Western residents and travelers gather in the early morning quiet, to read their papers and look past the city walls to the teak forests and mountains beyond.

Over tea and a fresh-baked scone I watch the city awaken. Trishaw drivers pedal past, street vendors set up their pushcarts. I resolve to keep to myself in Chiang Mai, to spend my time here writing and reflecting, not seeking out other travelers. With so little time left in Asia, I want to take full advantage of the learning opportunities I'd passed by earlier along the way.

The guest house Lin recommended is perfect, on a ridge above the moat, with a view over the Old City walls to the river beyond.

Hours before check-in, the manager hands me a carved teak elephant, palm-sized, attached to a huge, brass room key that would be difficult to misplace. Guests are to leave their elephants at the desk whenever they go out, so he'll always know who has left the building. When everyone has returned for the night, the massive front gate will be locked, and silence is the rule.

The centuries-old building is well-weathered, with the peaked tile roofs of antiquity, but the room is spotless and modern. There's a dial phone, even a bathtub that I loll in most of the morning, only to emerge when some song lyrics I've been groping for hit me.

In homage to the yodeling Texan I've been working on a country tune, sung with a twang, called *The Ballad of Mike and Lin.* I'd gotten the melody and first verse in Penang, when we'd all met, the second in Koh Samui, and now, in Chiang Mai, I'm getting the last. My songs usually have three verses. Kind of like life, I'll realize much later, while I am remembering Southeast Asia. It's a three-act play. Beginning, middle, end, and no matter how young I feel, or look, or behave, as of my next birthday there will be no denying that Act III is about to begin.

AT NOON I LEAVE MY ELEPHANT at the front desk to the old walled city. Hardly any cars go by, the occasional tuk-tuk or trishaw, not much traffic.

I come across Lin's top restaurant recommendation and instantly develop a yen for Japanese food. The place must be good, there's authentic fake-plastic food in the window.

Inside I'm seated beside a rowdy Thai foursome, a girl and three guys who are passing a bottle of Mekhong around under the table, pouring shots in their teacups. The men are having a rollicking good time. The girl looks like she'd rather be somewhere else.

One of them notices me, smiles and raises his teacup filled with whiskey.

I smile and raise mine. *"Chok dee!"*

Everyone turns. *"Pood Thai?"* asks the one at the head of the table.

A little, I answer. *"Nit noi."*

"I speak Ingrish. You come sit with us!" He pulls a chair over next to him while the other two guys chant *sit with us*: *"Nung kob re! Nung kob re!"*

So much for keeping to myself in Chiang Mai. I've been adopted.

The portly guy at the head of the table, Mr. Boon Me, introduces me to the others.

"This, Raj." Not Mr. Raj. Maybe relatives. "This, Mr. Yao. This"— he nods to the bored-looking girl—"bride of Mr. Yao! They have just marry!"

"Newlyweds!" I raise my teacup. *"Mazel tov!"*

The girl scowls, conveying the impression she might not have not chosen to spend her honeymoon on a drunken bender with her husband's buddies.

Through my interpreter Mr. Boon Me, I tell the group about all the places I've seen, including my visit with the Karen.

The bride jerks to attention. *"Mæ khong chan Karen!"*

"Your mother is Karen?"

She nods and smiles, the only time she will during our brief acquaintance. An instant later she's frowning again. Her groom is passing a little vial of red liquid under the table which Mr. Boon Me pours into a teacup and offers me.

Everyone leans forward as I raise the cup and sniff. *Opium.* They're mixing narcotic cough syrup with their whiskey.

"*Mī dī!*" No good! I sputter, widening my eyes in an exaggerated show of shock and disapproval so they'll know I'm kidding. Everyone laughs. I sense I've passed initiation. No one pushes any food or drink on me after that. Instead, they start pushing Mr. Boon Me.

Mr. Yao gives me a sly look. "*Nay Boon Me hawcı khung kheā seīy.*"

Boon Me looks flustered and signals for the check.

"What'd he say?"

Boon Me sighs. "He say I tell you, my heart is broken."

As they egg him on, Boon Me reveals he recently proposed to a girl who'd turned him down. "She say, I am too fat!"

He mops his brow with a napkin, stands and pulls my seat out. He's close to my height, wearing a loose silk shirt intended to minimize his Buddha-esque paunch.

"*N'gein cæn-wun mak!*" Raj coaches him.

"He say, tell you I am rich." Boon Me gestures for me to precede him. "You want come with us up the mountain?"


At the entrance to Wat Doi Suthep stands one of the world's largest gongs. It sounds with an immense power that would not be considered loud, that is felt more than heard. It makes my bones vibrate.

"Mr. Boon Me," I ask. "What is the Thai word for God?"

"*De-wa-da,*" he intones. *Diva,* deity: all these words are related. That whole human family thing. "God."

The panoramic views of Chiang Mai and the surrounding countryside are amazing from here, a mountaintop home to a monastery that dates back to the 1300s and is reached either by way of a 360-step flight of stairs, or winding mountain paths that snake through a series of waterfalls.

We take the nature trail back down. We take photos in the mist, then I shoot the newlyweds on the rocks, like a society couple posing in Central Park for the Sunday New York Times—the wedding portrait they'll never see.

Back in town Mr. Boon Me invites me to join them for the evening. Two more men join us for dinner, both very sweet, and very drunk. This place has no Western clientele and the food packs major heat. I play it up big, sputtering, choking, fanning myself. This is how you make friends. Attempt the language, taste the food, act like you're dying; sure-fire ice-breakers.

After dinner we hit a nightclub where couples are gliding around gracefully in what looks like a cross between the waltz and the Texas two-step. Each man in our party tries to teach it to me, but these are sophisticated steps, ballroom moves, harder to pick up than our silly American disco dancing, not to mention the language barrier. I step on each of their toes in turn and one by one they give up, particularly since some pretty girls have arrived at the table to show them a good time.

The girls are on duty, of course, but they make an effort to include us women in the fun, teasing the guys, then rolling their eyes conspiratorially at us. *Men. Aren't they putzes?*

Everyone's unbelievably friendly. I'm the only *farang* in the place, and all night long people keep walking up to me, saying, Hello! No pood Ingrish!

That's OK, goes my stock reply, I don't speak Thai. *"Mî ben rì, chan mì pood Thai."*

"So happy you with us!" they tell me. "So happy you here!"

I think about home. What would a roomful of white Americans say to the only foreigner in the place, a non-English-speaking person of color? *So happy you here?*

I don't think so.

Everyone's having a great time except Mrs. Yao. She sits all night with her arms crossed, frowning, while dance-hall hostesses drape themselves all over her groom and spoon narcotic-spiked whiskey down his throat.

The next morning, hung over, I sign up for one of those mini-bus hill-tribe tours that includes a restaurant lunch and many stops at souvenir shops.

We're five Yanks on the bus—a 50-ish couple and two college guys studying abroad I peg for boyfriends. One of them is seriously grating on me by lunch, when he looks around for the waiter and says, I'd like some more tea, where is that *flaming queen* that was serving us, and I give him dirty look, and he's like, "What? You didn't notice?"

But later he redeems himself. We visit a Meo tribal settlement in the mountains above Chiang Mai. The Meo, says the guide, migrated most recently from Laos, though their origins are uncertain. They're a striking people, with light complexions, like the Karen, especially the children, wearing distinctively embroidered black clothes, with their hair twisted up in topknots and secured in headdresses of shocking pink.

We pull over at a school while the kids are at recess. Boys chase around the little playground, spinning tops or hurling small wooden balls at each other they catch in cups at the end of a stick. They're identical to the handmade wooden toys I'll later see Mayan children playing with in Guatemala.

Gay College Guy starts chatting with the teacher in a tonal language I can only identify as not Thai.

"What? You speak *MEO?*"

"Of course not," he says. "That was Mandarin."

"She speaks Mandarin?"

"Of course she does. Migratory people just—pick it up. Hill tribes typically speak three, four languages fluently. Their own tribal dialect, Thai, Hmong, Mandarin...." He pauses, watching my wheels turn.

"That's right. They speak four languages; we don't know shit. That's why I came here." Something catches his eye behind me. He jerks his chin for me to look. "Over there. See what that man's doing?"

I see a man tending his garden. "That guy watering his flowers?"

"Yes. See what kind they are?"

They're a brilliant red, a cheerful sight in the gray mist, the kind you put in your lapel on Veteran's Day. "Poppies, I guess." Oh. Wait. *Poppies.*

"That's right," he says, once I've connected the dots. "We're in the Golden Triangle. These tribes are the world's top heroin producers. It's how they maintain their way of life."

I think of the diversity of culture and ethnicity I've been exposed to: the languages, religious beliefs, music and art and cuisine, every bit of it endangered. But is this the only way they'll survive? Serving as photo-fodder for tour groups, observing them like in a people-zoo? Cultivating heroin?

"Oh God. I never thought about any of this when I first started out. I just wanted an adventure."

"Nothing wrong with that," he says.

"But then it sort of—turned into something else along the way."

He smiles. "Well then. Sounds like your adventure has been worthwhile."

Back at the guest house, there's a message from Mr. Boon Me. He'll be by to pick me up for a party tonight.

He arrives in a bicycle cab with an armload of roses, sweat beading on his upper lip in the cool evening.

*"Sowā dī tan yen."* He offers me the bouquet and helps me slip into my jean jacket. Boon Me sure has all the moves. He's well-mannered, wealthy, educated—why hasn't some Thai girl snapped him up by now?

*"Kob khun ka."* I bury my face in the roses, inhaling dewy droplets. This could get awkward. "They're beautiful."

The driver pedals us to a modern section outside the city walls. Boon Me tells me the Thai words for random objects we're passing, then falls silent.

I try to remember the word for God.

*"Dewa-da,"* Boon Me says. "God."

*"Dewa-da,"* I say, but not that he'd read my mind.

"Marry me," he says.

The party isn't at the restaurant or nightclub I'd expected.

It's in a suite of adjoining motel rooms, and the guests are a bunch of liquored-up Thai men who are not of Mr. Boon Me's genteel background. Some of them look like downright thugs. My stomach starts churning. I'm the only Westerner—that I expected—but I'm also the only woman.

Raj comes up to me, the only familiar face.

"WHERE ARE THE OTHERS?" I shout.

He shrugs. "No Ingrish."

I find Boon Me slamming a bathroom-tumbler full of Mekhong, sweating profusely.

"Where are our friends? Where's Mr. and Mrs. Yao?"

"They go home. Honeymoon OVER!" He knocks back the whiskey, then takes a swig from a silver flask filled with the red syrup. Boon Me is not a happy drunk. His courtly manner has gone belligerent. Sweat beads up on his snarling upper lip. His eyes have a creepy, hopped-up look. I'm scared to tell him I want to leave, but the prospect of staying is much scarier.

"Mr. Boon Me, I can't stay. I have to leave now."

"Go NOW?" He mops his face with a paper napkin. "We will no LEAVE! I ask you MARRY ME!"

I feel like I can't breathe, frantic and trapped. *Fear is the mind killer.* I dart towards a pair of sliding doors, Boon Me on my heels.

He snatches up the roses. "NO FORGET YOU FLOWERS!" he bellows.

Raj follows us outside.

"Where can I get a ride?" I ask him, pulse racing.

"No Ingrish!" Raj steps between me and Boon Me.

They get into a shouting match that turns physical; jabbing, pushing, gesturing at me. Raj, my defender, fit and sober, nimbly dodges pokes from Boon Me's chubby hands until finally the altercation ends with Boon Me stumbling back through the sliding doors, Raj close behind.

I remain outside holding the roses, trembling, my heart hammering: now what? *I will face my fear.*

Raj comes back with a shifty-eyed man who has long, greasy hair. They walk me to a pickup truck, Raj opens the door for me and gestures me to climb in, so I do, with the flowers. The other man slides into the driver's seat.

And then Raj, instead of climbing in beside me as I expected, closes the passenger door.

The shifty guy turns the ignition and jams the shift into first. "WAIT!" I scream. "RAJ!" I stick my head out the window. "AREN'T YOU COMING?"

The truck peels away.

My mouth dry and stomach in somersaults, I plaster myself against the car door, hand on the handle.

The man doesn't speak.

"I thought Raj was coming." Heart banging, temples throbbing, full panic mode.

"No pood Ingrish." He careens wildly through the streets, scattering the trishaw drivers, sending fresh spasms into my gut every time he glances my way. There's a horrifying series of high-speed turns, then he slams on the brakes at an intersection I recognize—the town square.

In the red glow of the stoplight he turns to look at me like a snake at a mouse.

My stomach turns to liquid. The man is literally scaring the shit out of me.

He grips the shift knob and guns the motor, I turn the door handle and sputter thanks, I can walk from here. I spring from the cab and sprint across the street to the café where I sipped tea that first morning and marveled at the tranquility of this lovely place. Two blond men are smoking and drinking out front, one big, the other huge. I rush to their table, yank out a chair and slide into it, trying to make myself invisible.

"I gotta sit here." Heart palpitating, stomach in spasms, doubled over, gasping for air.

"Lovely roses," the larger man says. He's German.

"It's dark out, you can take off your sunglasses," says the other German.

"They're prescription," I pant. "I can't see without them."

I pull my jean jacket over my head. "Is there a truck coming around the corner?" I ask, from beneath the jacket.

"No truck," one of them answers, then they sip their beers and resume conversing like I'm not there.

It's getting stuffy under the jacket, so I come up for air, taking this opportunity to moan a bit and clutch my gut. "Oh my God. OH MY GOD. Holy crap."

"Vot hoppened?" the smaller man inquires casually.

"I was at this party," I start off, to be immediately interrupted by a man storming up to the table.

"YOU!" He screams in the bigger man's face. "I AM REALLY GODDAMN PISSED AT YOU!" He's American, blond, and beautiful, a James Franciscus look-alike. "I CAN'T TAKE ANY MORE OF THIS SHIT!"

Then he stomps away, grumbling and swearing.

Neither German's expression changes. They resume conversing in their mother tongue.

From what I can pick up, the giant man has a plan to smuggle something out of Burma and the big one doesn't think it's such a great idea.

"I just came from Burma," I say. "Don't even think about it."

"*Sprechts du Deutsch?*"

"Yeah. They're not so nice to drug smugglers."

"I'm not talking about drugs." The man leans in. "I'm talking about gems. Rubies, emeralds, sapphires. Easily concealed."

Interesting. This plan has a certain degree of élan that running cartons of Marlboros into Rangoon and bringing heroin back out rather lacks. "Jewel smuggling?"

"They're not suspicious of women." The German seems to be warming to my presence, "How thoroughly were you searched in Rangoon?"

"Not at all. I crossed over from Mae Sot."

"That's not allowed," he says admiringly.

"Yeah, well, neither is smuggling."

He smiles. "You know that one good heist can set you up for...years."

"No way," I say. "*Nicht interessiert.*"

"*Ihre Aussprache ist sehr gut!*"

"*Danke schön,*" I say. "Got a cigarette?"

"*Ah, Scheisse,*" the other says. "*Er kommt zurück.*"

The handsome American has returned. "What'd you DO that for?"

"You sew them into the hem of your dress," the smuggler continues. "Basically foolproof."

The American mutters and walks away again.

"Not a chance," I say.

"YOU FUCKING IDIOT!" The American spins around, yanks a chair out and collapses into it like I did. "Now we're going to have to FIGHT those guys!" He slams his fist on the table.

"Don't be silly," the German says mildly. "It's nothing. It happened four months ago."

"THEY'RE LOOKING FOR US RIGHT NOW!" The American screams.

Finally he notices me. His perfect features light up. "Why, hel-*lo*," he trills. "What're *you* doing here?"

"She was running from someone in a truck," the big German explains, happy to change the subject.

"I was at this party with a bunch of Thai people."

The gorgeous Yank raises his hand. "Say no more. That explains it."

"Right." I say. "So I'm at this party..."

"I *said* that explains it. Say no more."

Looks like I'm never going to get to tell this story. "Whereya from," I sigh.

"Milwaukee."

"No kidding! I'm from Chicago. Milwaukee's a great town!"

"It stinks."

"I SIT HERE?" someone screams.

A Thai woman, drunk or drugged and extremely unsteady on her feet, has like me come to this table of large blond men seeking asylum.

Unlike me, however, she *has* been followed. Moments later several Thai men stagger up to the table, shouting. One starts yanking at her.

The smuggler pulls her chair close and puts his arm around her. "She's with us. Leave her alone."

Go home, the American screams. *"BI thī BAN."*

Come with us, they shout. *"Mā phram kob reā!"*

"She's staying right here," the German says. He's so immense he's intimidating even sitting down, speaking in normal conversational tones.

*"Bi cāk thī nī!"* the American yells.

"Yeah," says the huge man. "Get outta here."

Eventually they calm down and split and the American starts lecturing the girl in fluent Thai while she keeps crying and blubbering in what even I can tell is very slurred speech.

The big man attempts to comfort her, petting and stroking her, while oddly doing nothing to shut Milwaukee up.

"Lay off her, why don'tcha," I finally interrupt, weary of her drunken sobbing.

"You have any idea what I'm saying?" He pauses the diatribe to light a cigarette.

"Something about her sister."

"No," he says. "I called her 'little sister.' I'm trying to *help* her."

She clutches me. "Me no good oo-man," she says. "You *good* oo-man. Me no good. How old you?"

I tell her I'm 24.

"I 30," she says. "I drunk, no good." She looks around the table. "These men, no good. You go hotel, sleep alone. These men, no good."

I decide to take her excellent advice. "Good night all," I say, looking for a trishaw. "It's been real."

"Don't forget your flowers," the other German says.


I flag down a bicycle cab with a teenage driver who can't find my guesthouse. He speaks only three words of English— I love you—which he keeps repeating, at one point even climbing into the carriage and dropping to one knee. Under other circumstances I'd have found it sweet, but this is one delay too many for my upset stomach. PULL OVER, I scream, waving my arms, clutching my gut, but he doesn't seem to grasp the urgency and I end up heaving over the side of his carriage.

Now he's not so in love. He pedals into a gas station, asks for directions, speeds to the guesthouse, but it's way past curfew by this time and the gates are closed.

I button my jacket. This is going to be a long night.

Or is it?

I push against the gate. Thank God. One heavy door creaks. It hasn't been bolted.

And neither has the front door. I tiptoe into the lobby and there, awaiting me on the front desk, sits my elephant key.

I check out first thing in the morning, eager to return to Bangkok for some peace and quiet.

"Thank you for leaving the gate open," I tell the manager. He inclines slightly. I have received several calls from Nay Boon Me, he says, but he thought I would not want to be awakened.

I incline deeply. *"Kob khun ka."*

*"Mì ben rì.* Today you go see elephants?"

Watching elephants pretend to carry logs is one of Chiang Mai's popular tourist pastimes. Okay, they're not pretending. They're actually carrying the logs—the same logs every day—a fact that surely can't be lost on the elephants. Afterwards, people who opt to may ride the elephants, before being taken to another souvenir store.

I think I'll stick to a bike, I say. Stay well. *"Sawā dī."*

He bows: go well. *"Bī di^dī:"*

So I end up meeting an elephant.

Not one of the pretend workers, this elephant is gainfully employed on a plantation outside Chiang Mai.

A fellow is supervising a crew from atop him, the humans clearing scrub while the pachyderm takes on the more firmly-rooted vegetation.

The young man dismounts and brushes off his pants as I ride up. He looks about 20, with *kopi susu* coloring and dark almond eyes.

"Hi! You a Yank?" They can always tell. "You're a long way from town on a push-bike."

"It's my last day here. I'm just riding around taking pictures till my bus leaves."

Stepping closer, his face lights up.. My little silver Star of David, almost always concealed, has slipped from behind my tank top.

"You are—this kind of person?" No one has ever noticed or commented on it before. "I worked for one of your kind," he says. "A very nice man. Mr. Weinstein. He helped me get into college."

"Weinstein, of course."

"You KNOW him?"

"No! Just..."

"Oh." He laughs. "This must be a common name among your people." He introduces me to his elephant. "This is Ming Kwan. Would you like to ride him?"

"Um..." It's not just their girth. Elephants are very tall and I'm not good with heights. Plus, he doesn't smell so great. "Looks like he's having lunch."

Ming Kwan finishes the banana tree he's been nibbling at and thoughtfully appraises the shrubbery.

"He wouldn't mind. But all right, let's just take your picture with him then." He reaches for my camera.

I take one nervous step.

He seems puzzled, almost offended by my reticence so I force myself to inch closer, until we're both in the frame.

Just before he snaps the shutter I work up the nerve to reach out and pat the big fella.


My new friend serves me some tea in a plantation outbuilding. It's dark and cool inside, empty but for an official framed portrait of the King.

"I've seen this picture in every building in Thailand," I tell him.

"Of course." He places his hand over his heart. "We *love* our King."

223

It's difficult for me to conceive, but I do believe the Thai depth of feeling for their monarch is genuine.

Rama IX, King Bhumibol, will reign for 70 years.

He will live to become the world's longest-serving head of state.

He will not institute the religious reforms of his great-grandfather Mongkut, or the educational and social programs of his grandfather Chulalongkorn.

His politics will not always bear close inspection, but he is a father figure to his country, respected and revered, and when he passes, he will be dearly mourned.

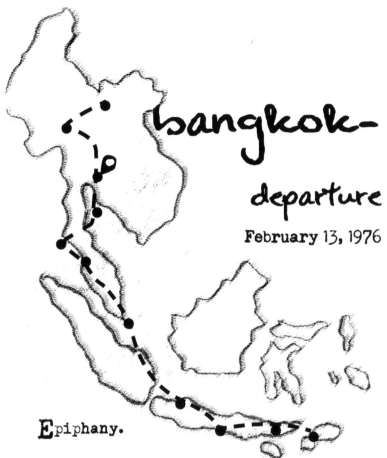

**bangkok—**

*departure*

February 13, 1976

**E**piphany.

Mike and Lin and I spend their last day in Asia wandering along the *klang,* watching the river homes bob in the current until the sun dips below the banyan trees.

Back at the hotel, organizing their luggage, Lin picks up her barber scissors. "Want one more haircut before I pack these?"

Mike rolls some blueprints into a tube. "Just give her a trim."

Both our heads turn. Cowboy Mike, involving himself in this girlie stuff?

He shrugs. "You got real nice hair."

This is the sole indication he'd ever noticed the first thing about my appearance. I hope Lin doesn't see how flattered I am.

If she does, she's too cool to care. She drapes me in a towel and starts snipping. "Don't put those blueprints away. Show her the house."

We pore over several layers of thin tissue overlays— bona fide architectural renderings Mike designed and drew up—the outdoor elevation, interior framing, plumbing and electric, and some systems I'll recognize later as far ahead of their time.

"See here? Speakers 'n lights all wired to this panel. Say the kids are raisin' a ruckus after bedtime—we'll just flip this switch 'n tell 'em, 'pipe down, lights out!'"

I look at Lin. *Kids?* A flush covers her freckles.

This is a great segue to my final tribute. "Okay, listen you guys." I pick up the guitar. "I wrote you a song. This house is even in it."

I hand them the sheet on which I've neatly penned the lyrics and chords for them to keep, and launch into *The Ballad of Mike and Lin* in the finger-pickin' key of C:

> *He was a long-legged Texas boy~*
> *She was a pretty little blue-eyed lady from the West...*

When I finish Mike's shaking his head, eyes glistening, hand over his heart, and Lin's crossing the room, arms outstretched, tears running down her cheeks, we're hugging and we're crying, *no one's ever done something like that for us,* she says, and wipes her eyes, then flashes those cute damn dimples, one last time.


After they've gone I hang around the pool, paralyzed by the heat, emotions in a jumble, anxious to move on, reluctant to leave. *I feel like I could go back to Bali and start all over again, I* write in the journal, then shuffle inside where it's cool.

There's a message. Jeffrey's in town, on the leave the Colonel had promised. *Let's go hear some jazz.*

He arrives at 7 on the dot, doused in after-shave. In a print silk shirt and khakis, with his hair slicked back, Jeffrey's looks somehow do not captivate me quite as they did in Mae Ta Wah. So there really *is* something about a man in uniform, I'm embarrassed to admit to my pacifist self. Am I reverting to some outmoded notion of men as protectors? Or does Jeffrey just look really cute in a beret? Hard to say.

On the way to the jazz club I ask about Peter.

"He's fine. Working hard on his film. He said to tell you he misses you."

I tear up and look away.

"Oh my goodness, I didn't mean to upset you! You'll be seeing him soon enough, I'm sure."

Big sigh. "No. We won't be seeing each other again."

Jeffrey stops short. "What do you mean? Have the two of you split up?"

I shake my head. "We were never together. We really just met. In Penang." *Six weeks and two days ago.*

"Is that so?" He looks shocked. "I thought you two were... engaged."

*Engaged. Imagine.* "No, it was just one of those things. On the road." I look at him. "You know?"

He nods. "I see. I didn't realize."


We're on the top floor of a hotel overlooking Bangkok, a beautiful city at night, with the golden wats glowing and the houseboats on the *klang* twinkling.

There's the tinkling of ice cubes against glass, muted cocktail lounge chatter, and on a riser a silver-haired Burman in dark glasses is tickling the ivories—real ivories—of an ebony baby grand.

Jeffrey puts his hands on the man's shoulders, leans down and says directly in his ear, "George! Guess who?"

George doesn't turn around. "JEFFREY!" He laughs heartily and does a special flourish on the piano by way of welcome. "Can you give us a set?"

"Try and stop me." Jeffrey signals the guitar player that he's going to sit in. "I've brought a friend." He pulls me closer. "A beautiful American girl. A musician!"

Another flourish. "A pretty girl is like a melody." George signals a server with his treble hand and keeps the bass walking. "Drinks on the house!"

"Bless his heart, he recognized my voice." Jeffrey knocks back a double Mekhong on the rocks, then steps up beside George to sing and play.

They do standards, some R&B, show tunes, trading phrases; they improvise, then return to the original melody, until finally George rocks forward into the final chord and nods to Jeffrey to take the last few bars, instrumental masters in perfect sync.

Jeffrey comes offstage to applause. He slams another double, then flushed and dreamy-eyed, whispers in my ear. "I love you, my darling."

He leaps back onstage, and he plays more, and he drinks more, and by the time we're back at the Federal, he's in a whirl of alcohol-and-jazz fueled emotion.

"I love you with all my heart," he says. "I could be happy with you for the rest of my life."

"Come on, Jeffrey. It's the Mekhong talking."

"It is not." He leans closer. "Be my wife. I will be faithful to you until death parts us."

What are the right words when a man you respect and admire, a man you care about, but not the way he cares for you, says everything you've dreamed of hearing—someday, from the right someone?

"Jeffrey, I... I think the world of you. You know that. But we're not... meant for each other."

"I understand." He adopts a peculiar posture. "You have your home, your life, and I am, after all, an inferior. A simple rebel."

I look at my friend. My talented, brilliant, courageous, principled, handsome, drunk-on-his-ass friend. Inferior? No. He doesn't get to play this card with me.

"You know that's not it. We're just headed in different directions. You have…" I'm groping. "A calling. A purpose."

He assumes a soldierly stance. "Yes. My people, our struggle. I have pledged them my life."

He asks for my picture. I give him a passport photo, and one Lin took of me giggling, trapped on the log at the water hole in Penang, just before I fell over, and he asks me to inscribe it.

On the back I write: *For Jeffrey—Remembering the rebel. Always, C.*

He looks disappointed, but he slips the photo into his shirt pocket and lays his hand over it. "For as long as I live, until I die, this picture will be on my body."


FORTY YEARS LATER, on a cold Chicago morning, I'll watch the falling snow and remember Jeffrey, his future ahead of him on that hot Bangkok night. How he'd asked, *may I kiss you?*

And how I'd felt swept away in the romance of a brave man going to war thinking of me, and he'd taken me in his arms for a movie kiss: prolonged, dramatic, yet perfectly chaste, just like the kisses he'd seen on the silver screens of his boyhood, when Rangoon was the cinema capital of Southeast Asia.

# chicago

March 6, 2016

# Symmetry

The Boeing 707 departed Bangkok after midnight, the same time I arrived in Bali, the same plane. That appealed to me. Balance always has. I like even numbers, pictures hung straight, songs in 4/4 time, verses that rhyme—so the symmetry, the *sameness,* in the way the journey began and ended, was pleasing to me, then and now.

That the journey had changed me, beneath the surface, hidden from view, appealed to me too. I knew I'd evolved—from tourist to traveler, novice to expert—now I would add, from child to adult. I guess we don't realize we're coming of age while it's happening, it only occurs to us in retrospect.

I've never enjoyed flying but I've always liked airports, especially back then, when people looked at each other instead of their screens.

I watched a black US serviceman and his Thai wife coax giggles out of their crying baby, a Sikh family explore the terminal in single file, a group of Filipinos shiver in the air-conditioning as they headed to jobs as 'guest' workers in Qatar, Lebanese businessmen in three-piece suits search for papers in their briefcases.

I was the only Western woman waiting to board, definitely the only passenger wearing a jean jacket with a guitar and army-surplus backpack over her shoulders, and surely the only person in the airport who became very emotional in the ladies' room, staring at an electric hand-dryer that bore the nameplate *World Dryer Manufacturing Company—Chicago, Illinois.*

Back at the gate, where we passed through no metal detector, our bags were not searched and our seats were not assigned—I fidgeted, checked my ticket and Traveler's Cheques and flipped through my passport. Many more pages to fill.

Finally a smartly uniformed Jordanian woman tapped the microphone and called the flight for boarding.

I slipped on my backpack, fixed my guitar over my shoulder and took my place in line as piped-in muzak played the theme song from Bonanza.

Thomas Mann had it backwards, I decided as I walked through the jetway towards the rest of my life. You can't *leave* home.

I ARRIVED HOME IN APRIL, intending to leave soon after. I was going to write music, play in clubs, be an ex-pat. I worked temp office jobs and open-mike nights. The plan was to save up a little more, bank my 1975 tax return and take off again, to send home more tri-folded self-stamped mailers marked *Par Avion.*

Even after a girlfriend gave some guy my number, even after he called and said, *we're going to the same party tonight, would you like a lift,* even after I married him and resumed my career-ladder climb, I never abandoned this plan. It just kept getting postponed.

I've never left Chicago.

I've gone from wife to mother, from backpack to briefcase, from apartment to house, but I kept traveling, for reasons both business and personal. Alone, with my colleagues, then my staff; visiting client headquarters and staying in executive suites, or alone, with my husband, then our kids, visiting exotic locales and staying in budget lodgings.

One morning I opened the door to my corner office and thought, I never expected to end up here. Then I remembered having the exact same thought so many years earlier, in a sleeping bag in a jungle in Burma.

I had always stayed somewhat informed on that situation. In 1990, *Time* ran a piece on the Karen entitled *Child Warriors,* that depicted a 13-year-old boy soldier on the cover.

Within, a photo captioned *Camp Near Thai Border,* practically stopped my heart. It had been taken, unmistakably, in the barracks in Mae Ta Wah, where the boys slept head to foot on straw mats.

The room looked just the same, the boys looked just the same; there was only one difference—a small TV propped up on a wooden crate.

A silver-haired man sat in the only chair, his face in shadows and his back to the camera. I told myself this man was Jeffrey, that here was proof he was safe and well.

As THE 40TH ANNIVERSARY of this journey approached, I set off on another one, to retrace my steps and record my recollections, to research the places I'd been, the people I'd encountered; to fill in the blanks. Facts and connections that had eluded me came to light: so *that's* what tribe they were from—what river we were on—how I got sick—why he looked at me that way.

For now, I had not only the wisdom of years but the tools of the 21st century at my disposal, tools much more powerful than magazines left lying in reception rooms. I had the modern-day Akasha, God's brain; the Internet.

I could zoom in on street views of Penang's Sunset Beach, I could surf listings for luxury villas in Koh Samui.

I could even look up my old friends.

I tracked them all down, my closest comrades. I learned of their accomplishments, saw pictures of their spouses, their children and grandchildren, their homes. I pored over social media profiles, corporate websites, court transcripts, and sadly, one obituary.

I scanned and restored my old photos, and the picture of the camp in Mae Ta Wah I'd torn out of Time magazine.

When I enlarged it, I noticed something I hadn't before. The man in the chair was holding the TV remote. That was a comforting thought—the boys watching videos before lights out, Jeffrey having himself a little nip of Mekhong after they fell asleep.

But surely Jeffrey was destined for bigger things than rewinding videos for the boy soldiers in camp.

On the 67th anniversary of the Resistance, January 31st, 2016, I researched the history of the Karen.

Their first recorded contact with the West was in 1827. Missionaries described them as unusually light-skinned and noted that unlike the other animist tribes in the region, they were monotheists.

Their belief in one God had been passed down in oral tradition from generation to generation. He was their Creator, and they called him *Y'Wa*.

My hand holding a coffee cup froze in mid-air, like Jeffrey's holding the bamboo whiskey tumbler. *Y'Wa*. In Hebrew: *Yahweh*.

*Y'Wa* had placed his first children in a beautiful garden and given them fruit to eat but forbade them to partake of one in particular. Then a serpent convinced them to eat the forbidden fruit. They were evicted from Paradise.

The legends told of a Book of Gold *Y'Wa* had given to a group of brothers, because *Y'Wa* loved them above all others, because they were his Chosen. The book contained the Word of *Y'Wa*.

The eldest brother, a Karen, refused to learn to read The Book and rejected its teachings. But the youngest, described as the lightest-skinned of the brothers, learned to read The Book and vowed to live in accordance with its principles.

He left the country of his elder brothers and prospered. But according to prophesy, he would one day return—with The Book. This time the Karen people would learn to read The Book, and they too would prosper.

Some scholars theorized Christian wanderers had contact with the Karen before 1827. Others disagreed. Christian missionaries would surely have introduced the teachings of Jesus and the New Testament.

These legends were confined to the Five Books of Moses; these people called their Creator by the same name as the Hebrews.

Might the Karen be one of the Lost Tribes, the descendants of one of those older brothers we children of Levi and Judah keep searching for and hoping to find?

This explained why the Sgaw Karen had so readily converted to Christianity. All was as had been foretold: the light-skinned brother had returned with The Book—along with its sequel—and in accepting Y'Wa's Word the Christians had risen to the top of Karen hierarchy to hold all the positions of power. Then it all backfired.

Citing an imbalance of authority, the Buddhist Karen majority split off from the Christian-dominated KNLA and formed the Democratic Karen Buddhist Army. Now the Karen are fighting not only against the Burmans, but amongst themselves.

I never knew Jeffrey's last name. I searched on these terms: Jeffrey Sgaw Christian Karen—every descriptor I knew of him—and was immediately directed to an account on the *Amnesty International* site:

### Extrajudicial killing of Jeffrey Win.

On the night of 9 February 1995, at about 8.45 p.m., seven DKBA soldiers entered Mae La refugee camp in Tha Song Yang district, Tak province. They abducted four people from two houses, [including] Jeffrey Win, about 52 years old, deputy KNU judicial officer for Hpa-An district and the only Christian among the four.

All four were abducted at gunpoint and their hands bound. Jeffrey Win fought back and tried to escape but was shot and killed by the DKBA. Phado Jeffrey Win, a Christian of Sgaw Karen ethnicity, was married with one daughter.

Jeffrey would have been 52 in 1995.

My stomach tumbled into free fall; even as my mind argued another 52-year-old Sgaw Christian Karen named Jeffrey might hold a prominent position with the KNU, my gut knew the man they murdered was my friend.

I tried to verify.

I phoned a missionary who worked among the Karen, I tweeted relief organizations.

I even emailed photos of the Colonel, the Major and Jeffrey to the General Secretary of the Karen National Union, Naw Zipporah Sein, a heroine to her people.

Zipporah was the wife of Moses. *There are legends...*

I have never received a reply.

Still, I fantasize one day I'll receive an email with this subject line: *I think you knew my father.*


I have no plans to visit Southeast Asia again, though I easily could.

I guess I'd rather remember it as it was—when bicycle cabbies hauled their fares, and longboats bobbed at sea, and wooden houses on stilts lined the beaches.

I also haven't contacted any of my old friends, though I easily could.

For I am one who will always choose to imagine.

And in my mind, in my heart, they're still out there—still on the road, still in their twenties, in the mine of magic time.

# To the Reader

Thank you for joining me on this journey to another time and place. Reconstructing and sharing this story so many years later has been quite a trip in itself, and it's been great having you along with me.

If *Overland* resonated with you and you have a moment to spare, would you consider leaving a short review on the page or site where you bought the book.? Your help in spreading the word is greatly appreciated. Reviews from readers like you make a huge difference in helping audiences and authors connect.

All the best,

~ cg

p.s. If you'd like to know when my next book comes out, or just feel like getting in touch, drop me a line: **caryn@manitou-cedarpress.com**

# Discussion Guide

While Overland at its core is a personal coming-of-age story, the historic, societal and political themes it incorporates suggest a number of topics for discussion. Below are some prompts.

***The political climate:*** Traveling abroad during a period of high anti-American sentiment was a highly confrontational exercise. Have you had a similar experience, either then or more recently? How did you handle it? How is today's political situation affecting international travel?

***Nationalism/Patriotism:*** The author makes sweeping generalizations about the characteristics of the different nationalities she encounters; were they offensive? Were such observations more acceptable before political correctness ruled? Does foreign travel instill either nationalism or patriotism in you, and how are they different?

***Colonialism:*** With the noted exception of Thailand, the countries along the author's route were under colonial rule as recently as the 1960s; virtually everyone she came in contact with had grown up under European domination. Are you conscious of feeling "Western guilt" when traveling in developing countries? Are colonialism's effects still apparent?

***Gender dynamics:*** The mid-1970s were a period of transition for a generation raised in traditional households but which matured during the sexual revolution. The author accepts men in traditional roles when it suits her but resents being treated as a subordinate; she dismisses objectification by men as "their problem."

# Discussion Guide

**Gender dynamics: (Continued).** Are these contradictions the author's personal issues, or are they typical of someone her age? Time period? How do these seeming contradictions resonate with your own experience?

**Backpack travel:** The ability to endure harsh conditions was a badge of honor on the Overland Trail and in keeping with the hippie ethic. Does the idea of lodging with families in homes with no electricity or running water intrigue or repel you? How far would you push your boundaries to have an authentic experience?

**Off the grid:** Would you have been able to tolerate the lack of communication and connectedness with family and the outside world that the author describes? Have you ever traveled in such a vacuum, or could you? Has technology made independent travelers less self-reliant, or is it simply a tool that enhances the modern travel experience?

**Counterculture critique:** Overland is a snapshot of the counterculture lifestyle with all its attributes: liberal politics, experimentation with sex and drugs, curiosity about Eastern religions and plenty of rock and roll. How closely does the author's experience jive with either your recollection or perception of the era?

**Reconnecting:** In the process of researching the book, the author tracks down her closest comrades via social media but chooses not to contact them. She also makes no effort to disguise their identities. Would you make those same choices?

# Author

Caryn Green is a media business veteran and time traveler based in 21st century Chicago.

She covers topics ranging from destinations, the arts and lifestyle to publishing, religion and the environment for various defunct and still extant print and online channels. *OVERLAND* is her first book.

*Jogjakarta December, 1975*

# Acknowledgments

Writing a book can be a solitary exercise. Or it can take a village, and that's way more fun. I'm indebted to my instructors and writing colleagues at the Iowa Summer Writer's Festival, the UW-Madison's Writer's Institute, Chicago's Story Studio and the Off-Campus Writer's Workshop for all their encouragement and guidance, and my special gratitude goes to my book club and beta readers; you were instrumental in this story coming to light.

Made in the USA
Monee, IL
29 November 2019